COMMON SENSE
ZONING
PRACTICAL SOLUTIONS FOR SMALLER CITIES

CONNOR MURPHY

Common Sense Zoning: Practical Solutions for Smaller Cities

Published by Wheatmark®
2030 East Speedway Boulevard, Suite 106
Tucson, Arizona 85719 USA
www.wheatmark.com

ISBN: 978-1-62787-736-7 (paperback)
ISBN: 978-1-62787-737-4 (ebook)
LCCN: 2019909078

Bulk ordering discounts are available through Wheatmark, Inc. For more information, email orders@wheatmark.com or call 1-888-934-0888.

for Paige

TABLE OF CONTENTS

INTRODUCTION
THE CHALLENGE OFFERED

A family member who lives in the city of Los Angeles recently asked me what I knew about the proposal to revise Los Angeles's outdated zoning. I told him I knew nothing about it—why would I? Nevertheless, I agreed to take a look at the Los Angeles proposal and give him some feedback; I've been a planner since 1972, so it would have been difficult to tell him I was the wrong family member to ask.

The next day, I went on the web and found the official City of Los Angeles Municipal Code.[1]

While I was snooping around on the internet, I decided I might as well look up a couple of facts about Los Angeles:

- "The nation's most densely populated urbanized area is Los Angeles–Long Beach–Anaheim, Calif., with nearly 7,000 people per square mile.[2]
- Los Angeles itself had a 2016 population of 3,976,322, and it is still growing. In fact, the city of Los Angeles has grown larger every year since its founding in 1781.[3]

CITY OF LOS ANGELES ZONING CODE

Los Angeles's zoning was adopted in 1946 and amended innumerable times over the past seventy or so years.

The original zoning provisions were 84 pages long, and the current edition of the zoning provisions is over 600 pages long. It's so long, city hall can't keep track of the exact number of pages—regulatory bloat.

RE:CODE LA PROJECT TIMELINE

Looking through the Los Angeles *re:code LA* project pamphlets and brochures, I found that the zoning code rewrite started in 2013 and was scheduled to end in 2017. That's five long years. But it is now 2019, and re:code LA is still dragging on.

I don't suppose anyone can say for sure when or if it will ever be completed.

Had I been assigned the task of scheduling the rewrite, I think I would have substantially reduced the timeline for completing the work and limited the work to cleaning up the existing code—not expanded the work to include even more material. Los Angeles is making the dangerous assumption that the zoning code *re:code* can solve all manner of urban problems, from aesthetics to traffic congestion.

Experience working as a city planner has taught me that zoning is not all that powerful; zoning has real limitations.

I was immediately struck with a question: How could Los Angeles spend so much time revising their out-of-date zoning provisions?

Then, when I read that Los Angeles had agreed to spend $5 million revising their out-of-date zoning provisions, I was immediately struck (or dumbstruck) with a second question: Why would Los Angeles spend so much money?

HOW? WHY?

Suddenly, I found myself being drawn into what my education and experience told me was an intellectual black hole. But my lifelong curiosity took hold of me and needled me into becoming an unwilling participant unable to ignore the disturbingly overoptimistic Los Angeles *re:code LA* project.

Now I've gone beyond mere curiosity; I'm committed to answering my own questions: How? Why?

Chapter 1

THE CHALLENGE ACCEPTED

I was baffled by a puzzling question: How could Los Angeles spend so much time and money rewriting their land use regulations?

ZONE LIKE WE MEAN IT

One of the *re:code LA* pamphlets says, "Let's zone like we mean it, in a transparent way. No more using industrial zones to build shopping centers, no more special zone change conditions on top of overlays on top of outdated base zones."[4]

SAY IT LIKE WE MEAN IT

The term *re:code LA* is a spiffy advertising slogan. But what does *re:code* mean? It means nothing at all. All a code is is a logical organization of ordinances. It has nothing to do with content. The real name is "code of ordinances." You could, I suppose, call it "a filing cabinet full of ordinances," "an ordinance filing cabinet," or "a book chock-full of ordinances." I suppose you could call your bedroom wardrobe "a code of underwear."

When Los Angeles said it needed to "recode," what city hall should have said was, "We need to rewrite our inadequate, out-of-date, and undecipherable zoning provisions."

Los Angeles doesn't have a problem with its code of ordinances; it has a problem with the English language. Los Angeles needs to improve its writing skills.

LAND USE REGULATIONS

From this point on, I'm going to stop using the term "zoning provisions" and start using a more descriptive term, "land use regulations." If you want, you may still use the slang term "zoning code."

Anyone who takes the time to read the current Los Angeles land use regulations will soon realize that the half-century-old document is so poorly written it couldn't possibly serve the best interests of the community—and probably never did.

But I'll confess, I haven't read all 600-plus pages from cover to cover. There is a limit to how much grammatical abuse I can stomach.

ONE SIZE FITS NONE?

Many jurisdictions, including Los Angeles, believe that as the population grows, land use regulations must also grow to keep pace. Make sense to you? Not to me.

Let's look at some comparisons:

- The city of Los Angeles, with a population of just about four million,[5] has land use regulations that are more than 600 pages long. Los Angeles encompasses a seaport, a former river, mountains, and earthquake faults.

- The city of Fresno, with a population of just over 500,000,[6] has land use regulations that are more than 1,200 pages long. Fresno, located in the heart of the San Joaquin Valley, is flat as a pancake, with only one geological feature: subsurface hardpan. Why are the Fresno land use regulations twice as long as the Los Angeles land use regulations?

- The generic land use regulations (subdivision and zoning)

used by cities of every size and shape, all across America, are only 153 pages long. Why are they so much shorter?

How can hundreds of other cities get by with 153 pages of land use regulations while Los Angeles needs 600 pages and Fresno needs 1,200 pages? The growth in pages alone, I would say, caused Los Angeles to end up with incomprehensible land use regulations.

HOLY GUACAMOLE

How about this for an explanation: Let's say the young Professor Cantinflas takes a position teaching English. At first, he only attracts 100 students to his classes. Professor Cantinflas teaches from *The Elements of Style*, by William Strunk, Jr., and E. B. White,[7] which is about 100 pages in length.

After ten years of teaching, the class load has grown to 1,000 students. Professor Cantinflas still teaches from *The Elements of Style*, which by Los Angeles's logic should have grown to 1,000 pages in length but is still only 100 pages in length.

After twenty years, the class load has grown to 10,000 students. Professor Cantinflas continues to teach from *The Elements of Style*, which is still 100 pages in length, but by Los Angeles's logic should have now grown to a colossal 10,000 pages.

Make sense to you? Not to me. Just because the number of students grows bigger doesn't mean *The Elements of Style* grows bigger just to keep pace.

In discussing population, one of the *re:code LA* publications says: "As a result [of population growth], LA's zoning code grew from 84 pages in 1946 to over 600 pages now."[8]

Make sense to you? Not to me. There is no connection between population and pages. Los Angeles is a collection of small towns that have coalesced; it's called a conglomerate.

Neither land area nor population dictates the size or complexity of land use regulations.

BEGINNING OF ZONING

In 1885, San Francisco "banned public laundries from most areas, a not-so-subtle attempt to zone the Chinese out."[9] Then, in 1909, Los Angeles adopted "a city-wide regulation that kept heavy industry and commerce out of certain neighborhoods."[10] These were the first two American attempts to separate land uses by zoning; neither amounted to much.

But, in 1916, New York City adopted America's first substantial zoning regulations.

The original twelve-page New York Zoning Resolution became the model for much of the local zoning that followed. Some of New York's experiments work well even today, while others have sent zoning ricocheting off in a near fatal trajectory.

- New York created zoning districts—" . . . residence districts, business districts, and unrestricted districts . . .
- New York created exclusionary zoning: "No building or premises shall be erected or used for any purpose other than a purpose permitted in the use district . . .
- New York created zoning districts that listed types of occupancy rather than structural types of building (grocery, hardware, clothing, etc.).
- New York created zoning districts that excluded odor, dust, smoke, gas, or noise (nuisances already addressed by existing police powers).
- New York created zoning districts that allowed mixed occupancy for no particular logical reason: "No use permitted in a residence district . . . shall be excluded from a business district.
- New York created exemptions for preexisting uses.

- New York created Height Districts . . . (a) one times districts; (b) one and one-quarter times districts (c) one and one-half times districts (d) two times districts, (e) two and one-half times districts."[11] (A height district connects building height to street width. For example, a one times district limits building height to one times the width of the street.)

MANY FLAWS

City planners have been stuck with all those New York conventions, both good and bad, ever since and have found it nearly impossible to shake free of some of the worst traps of the original New York Zoning Resolution.

Let's hope *re:code LA* can break loose from the traps that prevent the current Los Angeles land use regulations from fully meeting the needs of the community. For five million bucks, it should be a cinch.

SKIPPING THE FUNDAMENTALS

When I was in planning school, we zipped over zoning in one semester, as though we would never again come in contact with something so pedestrian during our planning careers—we didn't learn much about zoning because not much was taught to us. So, when I accepted the challenge of coming up with a better idea, I started my quest by looking up the planning curriculum at my alma mater, San José State University, in California. Surfing the net, I found a class called URBP 225: Land Use Planning and Law. The course description said, "Examination of the role of public law in addressing urban growth and environmental change issues, and the legal aspects of preparing and administering planning controls and incentives."[12] During a short four months, students study the interrelationship between the general plan, zoning regulations, and planning permits, as well as whether a land use action is legislative, adjudicative, or ministerial.

But that's not all; in the same class, students go on to study urban design and the urban environment, contemporary urban growth and the implications of major legal precedents, plus a lot more—all in the same class. It's enough subject matter to fry a student's brain but not spread out over enough time for a student to gain more than superficial knowledge.

When you do superficial teaching, you get superficial results. As historian and novelist Aleksandr Solzhenitsyn said, "Hastiness and superficiality are the psychic diseases of the twentieth century."[13]

Considering that most city planners spend their entire careers processing planning permits, a single semester (three hours a week for four months) doesn't seem to me to be adequate. Perhaps that is why, almost fifty years after graduating from planning school, I still see so many poorly written land use regulations.

PICK IT UP ON THE JOB

When I was in planning school, I asked the question, "When are we going to learn more about planning permits?" We never did learn more about planning permits. I was told we would pick it up on the job. I never did pick it up on the job, and I found out that nobody else did either. What I did pick up on the job was the wrong way to do the work. Inevitably, whenever I asked a colleague how I should process a planning permit application, I was told to go through the filing cabinets, pick out a previous application, and do the work the same way the previous planner had done it. So that is what I did. The results were most unsatisfactory. If the previous planner did it wrong, I too did it wrong. Most of my predecessors did it wrong. Fortunately, for most of my career, I was able to avoid processing planning permits, so I didn't have to worry about coming up with a better way to structure land use regulations.

In the next section, I am going to tell you a little about myself and about a special gift I have—a gift I am going to use throughout this book to figure out a better way to construct land use regulations.

THE GIFT OF HOLISTIC THINKING

Soon after graduating from high school, I was offered an opportunity to study electronics at a trade school in Germany. At eighteen, I had no idea what I was getting into or what it would be like going to school in a foreign country.

I soon found that German academic expectations were much tougher than what I had encountered in my small farm-town high school. The German school classes were taught by no-nonsense Prussian schoolmasters. I was also shaken to the core to find there was a pass-fail test every Friday afternoon. Those who passed the test moved on to the next week's lessons; those who failed didn't.

On the surface the curriculum looked simple enough; we were taught how to design and build electrical communications devices. Under the surface, however, we were taught systems thinking, the discipline that trains the mind to look beyond the obvious and see how what appears to be unrelated is actually part of a system.

SYSTEMS THINKING

The dictionary says, "Systems thinking is a holistic approach to analysis that focuses on the way that a system's constituent parts interrelate and how systems work over time and within the context of larger systems."[14]

I've never found an adequate way to explain systems thinking, but I can tell you that systems thinking takes over when the mind floats free and literally sees connections and interactions taking place. It's a useful skill to have when working with electrons.

I suppose I am also what they call a holistic thinker. I have always been a lousy student because I don't relate well to true-false or multiple-choice tests. I always have questions: What about the alternatives? How about the variables? I do great on essay tests, but not many teachers want to bother with them; they take too long to grade.

ACCIDENTAL ENCOUNTER OR SERENDIPITY

I suppose my accidental encounter with the *re:code LA* program, my lifelong curiosity, and my ability to engage in systems thinking or holistic thinking has guided me to where I am now, at the decision point where I feel I should come up with a logical system of land use regulations I can share with other planners, rather than continue to put up with the hodgepodge of unrelated folkways and taboos that presently pass for land use regulations.

REGULATIONS: FREE IS GOOD

I started my quest by looking at public domain land use regulations that are available to anyone willing to spend some time surfing the net.

From my initial research, I found that:

- most cities base their land use regulations on anonymous public domain land use regulations that have been floating around for decades; and
- many of the best land use regulations are free to anyone who wants to download them.

There is no reason for any jurisdiction, anywhere in America, to pay for reasonably good land use regulations.

Los Angeles is just wasting taxpayer money by believing in magical thinking or by hiring expensive consultants based on the belief that "the grass is always greener on the other side of the freeway."

Below is a list of reasonably priced sources Los Angeles could have used to put together a new set of land use regulations, but for some reason unknown to me, Los Angeles ignored the vast amount of inexpensive or free help available to it.

PAS Reports. The most important information for city planners comes from the Planners Advisory Service (PAS) of the American Planning Association (APA).[15] PAS has provided a wide variety of technical information for city and regional planners since 1949. PAS technical information is rarely seen by the general public because it is useful only to people actively engaged in urban planning research. Each PAS report covers a single planning subject, such as:

- Zoning as a Barrier to Multifamily Housing Development
- The Transportation/Land Use Connection
- Planned Unit Developments
- Planning Active Communities

Zoning Practice. *Zoning Practice* is a monthly publication that informs city planners and inspires smarter land use practice. It keeps its readers up to date on changing zoning laws across the country.

Longtin and Curtin. Anyone serious about understanding land use law in California, or any other state, needs to have access to two books:

Longtin's California Land Use[16]

Curtin's California Land Use and Planning Law (by Daniel J. Curtin, Jr., and Cecily T. Talbert; called "Curtin" in this book).[17]

Curtin is a well-known, often quoted, and definitive summary of planning laws, including expert commentary on the latest statutes and case law.

Trying to construct land use regulations without Longtin and Curtin at hand is a waste of effort. Curtin may be in your local library. Longtin is so specialized and expensive that you will probably have to buy your own copy. If money is an issue, Curtin is less expensive.

Texas Municipal Zoning Law. *Texas Municipal Zoning Law* is a book by John Mixon, James L. Dougherty, Jr., and Brenda McDonald that is useful for Texas municipalities only. There is a Kindle edition available. I have not read this book; the title is self-explanatory. I was surprised to find a planning book from Texas. Texas is not a planning mecca.

Subdivision Map Act Manual: A Desk Reference Covering California's Subdivision Laws and Processes. This is a book by Daniel J. Curtin, Jr., and Robert E. Merritt.

There is no reason to pay consultants $5 million to duplicate information available to any city hall that subscribes to the popular professional planning publications. Has Los Angeles ever heard of these low-cost publications?

ONE OUT OF 19,354

According to the U.S. Census, there are 19,354 incorporated places in the United States. You would think that out of all those cities, one of them would have land use regulations similar to what Los Angeles needs. Why didn't Los Angeles look around for land use regulations it could acquire from some other jurisdiction for free?

There is nothing so unique about the geography of La-La Land that would prevent it from using existing land use regulations from somewhere else.

DO WHAT WORKS

All that matters in the long run is that land use regulations do what they are supposed to do: segregate incompatible land uses; preserve traits that differentiate one neighborhood from other neighborhoods; prevent new development from lowering property values; and protect existing land uses from unwanted encroachment.

Unfortunately, after a lifetime dealing with land use, I'm no longer sure land use regulations actually do what they are supposed to do, nor am I sure land use regulations can ever be made effective; believing they can solve a wide range of urban problems is probably just magical thinking.

WIZARD OF OZ

Los Angeles has chosen to look outside of its Department of City Planning for leadership in reconstructing their land use regulations. That will probably turn out to be an unwise and expensive decision.

Believing that a wizard from afar can solve your local problems is just more magical thinking: "Pay no attention to the man behind the curtain."[18]

Outside consultants always pretend to be wizards who possess arcane knowledge, but behind the curtain, they are usually just little men good at selling overpriced or unneeded services to gullible public officials. Most of the time, outside consultants know far less than advertised.

LOCAL PLANNERS HAVE THE ANSWERS

In all but the most inimitable case, it is wiser to delegate problem-solving to the local planning staff and give them the resources to solve the problem.

Only a local planner who has been using the Los Angeles land use regulations on a daily basis over a long period of time would

- know where everything of importance is located in the land use regulations;
- know what land use provisions work well locally;
- know how to rearrange existing content to be more useful;

- know what content to eliminate because it isn't effective; and
- know what vital content is missing.

There is almost certainly a local planner on the Los Angeles planning staff who has for years been telling management what needs to be done and just how to do it, but management hubris has prevented anyone in authority from recognizing the local planner's problem-solving ability because the local planner is only a local. The local planner should be in charge of reconstructing the local land use regulations.

In America, it is common for management to disregard local talent in favor of outside wizardry.

What tipped me off to the existence of a local planner or two is the fact that planning permits have been more or less successfully processed for the past sixty years using the current zoning regulations. Obviously, at least one local planner in the Los Angeles Department of City Planning knows how to find things in the existing land use regulations. That is the local planner management needed to look for—but failed to do.[19]

Yeghig Keshishian, of the Los Angeles Planning Department says: We are nearly 400 employees strong. Together, we are the faces of Los Angeles City Planning. Covering 470 square miles and representing four million residents, we shape the future development of our City and its neighborhoods.[20]

In 1896, the Italian economist Vilfredo Pareto published *Cours d'économie politique*, a paper based on his observation that 20 percent of the peapods in his garden contained 80 percent of the peas.[21] Based on the Pareto Principle, eighty local planners in the Los Angeles Planning Department should be skilled enough to write new land use regulations. Why weren't they assigned the task?

Chapter 2
ADMINISTRATIVE OPTIONS

Anything the planning commission can do may also be done by the city council. A small, slow-growing jurisdiction doesn't need a planning commission. With little or nothing to do, the city council can act as the planning commission. In practice, however, most cities have a planning commission to take some of the workload off the city council.

As a jurisdiction grows, there will eventually be so many agenda items that a planning commission will become a necessary accessory to assist the city council in processing all of the agenda items.

ROLE IN PROCESSING PERMITS

The planning commission plays two roles in processing permits:
- The planning commission takes the place of the city council by approving or denying adjudicative permits.
- The planning commission acts as an advisory body by recommending the course of action the city council should take on approving or denying legislative permits.

MULTIPLE PLANNING COMMISSIONS

Eventually, if a jurisdiction becomes big enough, it may need more than one planning commission. Los Angeles has a citywide planning commission and seven subarea planning commissions.

The Area Planning Commissions (APC), each consisting of five private citizens who serve for a small attendance fee, largely serve as appeals boards for actions taken by the Department or the Zoning Administrator on such matters as conditional uses and variances. When authorized to do so by ordinance, the APCs also act as original decision-makers on some zoning matters and advise the City Planning Commission (CPC) and the Department on changes to the General Plan affecting their geographical areas.[22]

MULTIPLE SETS OF LAND USE REGULATIONS

Because big cities are conglomerates composed of many hamlets, villages, and small towns, they are municipal corporations, not places in which to live; people live in the neighborhoods located on both sides of the tracks—or freeways.

In the large jurisdictions I am familiar with, I've found that people living on one side of the tracks don't know and don't care what goes on on the other side of the tracks. People socialize and shop on their own side of the tracks; many fear or detest the people living on the other side of the tracks. Multiple sets of land use regulations just seem to me to be something a big city would want to have.

A jurisdiction doesn't start out big; it grows little by little by happenstance and leapfrogging, a situation where real estate developers bypass expensive land on the fringe of the jurisdiction and purchase cheaper land further out in the countryside.

Los Angeles started out as scores of small towns and unincorporated leapfrog real estate schemes that eventually ran up against each other in the absence of land use planning, goaded on by pure, unadulterated greed. (If you haven't seen the film *Chinatown*, you need to see it. *The Guardian's* film critic, Peter Bradshaw, said: "Chinatown is such a powerful piece of myth-making, a brilliant evocation of Los Angeles as a spiritual desert." Now, almost forty years after its 1974 release, Chinatown has been named the greatest film ever made.[23])

In megacities like Los Angeles, the scores of neighborhoods that developed during different decades have little in common. Residents are not likely to have any need to do business in other neighborhoods.

Whenever possible, local land use regulations should be written to meet the needs of neighborhoods. In 2019, the *Los Angeles Times* listed 272 neighborhoods for La-La Land.[24]

I don't see how a single set of land use regulations could be durable enough and flexible enough to meet the needs of all 272.

SECESSION MOVEMENT IN LOS ANGELES

Lack of attention and intimacy, on the other hand, can lead to divorce:

April 29, 2002—Three areas of Los Angeles—Hollywood, the Harbor area and the huge San Fernando Valley—are considering seceding from the city to form their own independent governments. Advocates of secession say smaller equals better.[25]

MEGALOMANIA?

Cities need to be big to feed big egos. A few years ago, the news media reported, "Los Angeles Mayor James Hahn opposes secession, and has raised $5 million to fight it. He and other opponents say that being part of the nation's second-largest city carries clout that smaller cities just don't have."[26]

Hahn let the cat out of the bag: "When you're from the city of Los Angeles, that says you're big right off the bat, and you need to be listened to."[27]

Former Los Angeles Mayor James Hahn reminds me of the Cold War classic, *The Day the Earth Stood Still*, where Tom Stevens (Hugh Marlowe), motivated by blind ambition, tells the government where it can find Klaatu (Michael Rennie). He believes that, by doing so, he will become, as he put it, "I'd be the biggest man in the country."[28]

ECONOMIES OF SCALE

Wikipedia says:

In microeconomics, economies of scale are the cost advantages that enterprises obtain due to their scale of operation (typically measured by amount of output produced), with cost per unit of output decreasing with increasing scale . . . Economies of scale often have limits, such as passing the optimum design point where costs per additional unit begin to increase.[29]

In regard to cities, there is no solid evidence to support the claim that big cities are more cost-efficient than small towns.

THE HERITAGE FOUNDATION STUDY

According to the Heritage Foundation:

Our analysis indicates that the Current Urban Planning Assumptions are of virtually no value in predicting local government expenditures per capita . . . [T]he actual data indicate that the lowest expenditures per capita tend to be in medium- and lower-density municipalities . . . ; medium- and faster-growing municipalities; and newer municipalities . . . It seems much more likely that the differences in municipal expenditures per capita are the result of political, rather than economic factors, especially the influence of special interests.[30]

Neither land area nor population determines the per capita cost of government.

THE NEWGEOGRAPHY STUDY

Wendell Cox, writing for NewGeography.com, tells us that "local government consolidation and regional governance is all the rage in policy circles," but there is no evidence that consolidation creates an economy of scale.[31]

The NewGeography study found that Pennsylvania's largest jurisdictions spent 150 percent more per capita than jurisdictions with populations of 5,000–10,000 and that New York's largest jurisdictions spent nearly 200 percent more per capita than such jurisdictions. The NewGeography study suggests this occurs because elected officials who know more of their constituents are likely to be more responsive to their needs.

The study also found that "America's small-town government structure engenders a sense of community, even as a part of larger metropolitan areas. They also save a lot of money because democracy works better when government is closer to home."[32]

The NewGeography study concluded, "It is not surprising that so many consolidation proposals fail and that when given the chance, voters usually reject consolidation proposals."[33]

TARGET AUDIENCE

Wendell Cox, writing for NewGeography.com, tells us that "America is more 'small town' than we often think. In 2000, slightly more than one-half of the nation's population lived in jurisdictions with fewer than 25,000 people."

Cox goes on to say, "According to the 2002 U.S. Census of Governments, there were more than 34,000 local general-purpose governments with less than 25,000 residents . . . . With so many 'small towns,' the average population of [incorporated places] in the United States are 6,200."[34]

MY KIND OF PEOPLE

Common Sense Zoning is targeted to appeal to those 34,000 small governments—governments that can't afford to hire pricey outside consultants or pay $5 million to update their land use regulations.

Chapter 3
ZONING OPTIONS

Most of this chapter is copied verbatim from my book, *Fight City Hall and Win: How to Defend Your Community Against Rapacious Developers, Scared Bureaucrats, and Corrupt Politicians.*

So, if you've read *Fight City Hall and Win,* you will find the following information to be familiar.

Zoning is a regulatory scheme used to control the use of real property (land and land-based structures). Zoning attempts to regulate at least three separate and unrelated aspects of real property—activities, structures, and appearance—and this leads to lengthy and complicated zoning ordinances.

REGULATING ACTIVITIES

Zoning regulates the activities that may be undertaken on a given property. For example, zoning may limit products that may be sold, hours of operation, or the means of satisfying desire (no sale of alcohol, no dancing, and no live music). Some say zoning takes the fun out of life.

REGULATING STRUCTURES

Zoning regulates the kinds of structures (residential or commercial) or their size, shape, height, and type. For example, zoning may require structures to be no taller than 20 feet, cover no more than 30 percent of a lot, or be set back from the property lines.

REGULATING APPEARANCE

Zoning serves to preserve the character of a neighborhood. For example, zoning may limit the exterior paint palette to protect sensitive eyes from visual blight and bad taste.

THE PLANNING-ZONING LINK

Planning and zoning are linked together in a chain. At the head of the chain are the three types of plans (the citywide plan, small area plans, and specific plans), arranged in a hierarchy, from most general to most specific. At the tail of the chain you will find zoning.

Zoning is the final and most specific link in the chain. Consequently, zoning is rigid and inflexible by design.

ZONING OR DIRT

When you invest in real property, you are purchasing zoning, not dirt. Zoning determines the comparative price of real property. Without the right kind of zoning, it might just be scenery.

PRIVATE ZONING

Zoning is imposed on a community by city hall, but there are also forms of private zoning-like rules called covenants, conditions, and restrictions (CC&Rs). CC&Rs are homeowner association rules imposed by the developer at the time of sale on the buyers to ensure they don't screw up the development before everything is sold. CC&Rs usually run for twenty years and may be extended by the property owners' association by a majority vote.

CC&Rs were often imposed in lieu of zoning from the 1920s through the 1940s, before zoning became widespread. Now CC&Rs

are imposed to maintain original appearance and prevent aesthetic deterioration and loss of property value. CC&Rs can apply to any form of real property development, from dwellings to industries. Whole neighborhoods can be covered by CC&Rs. Redevelopment agencies can add CC&Rs to real property in a project area to prevent a reversion to slum conditions. CC&Rs may specify acceptable exterior paint schemes, siding, roofing materials, and landscaping; they may also restrict building additions, parking, and storage of boats, campers, and junk.

CC&Rs are often thought to be limiting and frustrating, but they are safeguards that can make life better for law-abiding residents. They are class sensitive. Higher social classes tend to see them as protectors of property value and social decorum. Lower classes tend to see them as restrictions on personal rights. CC&Rs provide a level of social class protection that government is loath to impose through zoning. Neighborhoods that lack CC&Rs usually fall into decline because some people are determined to express their individuality by painting their property garish colors, removing landscaping, or parking what they call valuable collector cars in front yards and driveways.

EUCLIDEAN ZONING

Euclidean zoning is named after a famous court case, *Village of Euclid, Ohio* v. *Ambler Realty Company,* confirmed the legality of zoning. Euclidean zoning segregates land uses into geographically defined districts.[35]

PRIMARY USES

Typical land use zoning districts are the following:

- R-1 Single-Family Residential District
- R-2 Duplex (two-unit) Residential District
- R-3 Multiple-Family (three or more units) Residential District

- C-1 Neighborhood Commercial District (groceries, hardware and drug stores, banks, and the like)
- C-2 General Commercial District (downtown or the mall; consumer goods)
- M-1 Light Industrial District (consumer apparel, jewelry, instruments, computers)
- M-2 Heavy Industrial District (chemicals, steel, oil refining, mining)

EXCLUSIONARY USES

Uses allowed within one zoning district are "excluded"—not allowed—in all cases in other zoning districts. That is why homes are segregated from work and shopping. Euclidean zoning is often accused of creating American suburbia by promoting travel by automobile. However, by the dawn of zoning, in 1916, streetcar suburbs were already pushing urban growth out into the suburbs. In the early 1960s, the proliferation of suburban tract houses prompted Malvina Reynolds to write the hit tune "Little Boxes."[36]

ACCESSORY USES

Accessory uses are allowed in order to accommodate needs related to the primary uses. The following accessory uses are often allowed in an R-1 Single-Family Residential District:

- Home occupations and cottage industry
- Schools, public utilities, and quasi-public buildings
- Meetinghouses used for public assembly and especially for worship

DEVELOPMENT STANDARDS

Euclidean zoning also regulates dimensions, such as building setbacks from the property lines, height limits, and others.

The following standards are typical for an R-1 Single-Family Residential District:

- Minimum lot area: 6,000 square feet
- Minimum lot width: 60 feet
- Minimum lot depth: 100 feet

EUCLIDEAN ZONING INTENT

Euclidean zoning was originally intended to exclude noisy and smelly industrial uses, but it quickly devolved into pointless uniformity and rigid conformity. Most cities cling to Euclidean zoning because it is easy to administer, has a long history of legal precedent, and doesn't require hiring trained urban planners or design professionals to create or administer. Euclidean zoning is also simple enough for some (though not all) elected officials to grasp.

Euclidean zoning is often criticized for its lack of flexibility and its institutionalization of discredited primitive planning theory, but it doesn't always deserve its bad press, and there have been some successful attempts to make it less rigid.

PLANNED UNIT DEVELOPMENT

About sixty years ago, most cities added a flexible zoning district to ameliorate Euclidean zoning's inflexibility. The new zoning district is commonly called a planned unit development district (PUD). There is no universal agreement as to exactly what constitutes a planned unit development. My understanding of the concept suggests a PUD is a unified site development plan that integrates building design and surrounding landscape into the ecological setting with minimal impact. A PUD:

- takes creative advantage of the site's unique or unusual size, shape, topography, vegetation, natural characteristics, and relationship to surrounding land uses;

- blends housing design to suit a broad range of income and household characteristics;
- blends residential, commercial, and industrial land uses into a seamless unity; and
- combines multiple parcels to form a unified and aesthetically pleasing whole.

A planned unit development may be composed of one parcel or many parcels and may be under single ownership or multiple ownerships. Flexibility is its primary attribute.

EASY TO CRITICIZE

Euclidean zoning is often attacked as basically defective, when, in reality, most Euclidean zoning codes of ordinances suffer from writing deficiencies, not theoretical or technical ones. Good writing can solve most Euclidean zoning problems. Many land use regulations appear to have been written by monkeys jumping up and down on typewriter keys.

Some land use regulations are so poorly written they discourage creative development and promote bad development. Don't believe me? Try reading the City of Los Angeles Municipal Code. Euclidean zoning, augmented by planned unit development, is probably adequate for all but the most atypical cities.

INCENTIVE ZONING

Incentive zoning rewards applicants who are willing to give the government something the government wants for free, such as a new branch library, additional parkland, or low-income housing. Incentive zoning thus can get "nice stuff" for a community without public expenditure, but it can be difficult to administer fairly and objectively.

One Oregon jurisdiction requires all single-family residential lots to have a minimum area of 8,000 square feet. However, if an applicant is willing to build low-income housing, the jurisdiction grants an incentive by allowing the lot area to be reduced to 6,000 square feet.

PERFORMANCE ZONING

Lane Kendig, in *Performance Zoning*, tells us, "Performance zoning is a land use planning concept that has its roots in building codes that established performance standards as opposed to specification standards."[37]

Whereas Euclidean zoning would contain an absolute standard—"Floors and walls must be constructed of four-inch-thick masonry or stone"—performance zoning would contain a loose directive: "Floors and walls must be constructed so as to contain an interior fire for one hour."

Furthermore, performance zoning may also allow the applicant to deviate from planning standards by substituting desirable options, such as

- mitigating environmental impacts;
- providing public amenities; or
- building affordable housing.

Scholarly studies tend to suggest that the best zoning approach combines Euclidean zoning and performance zoning.

Proponents say performance zoning reduces the need to have many zoning districts, but it sounds to me that performance zoning is a zoning code with only one zoning district: planned unit development.

FORM-BASED CODE

According to the Form-Based Codes Institute: "A form-based code is a land development regulation that fosters predictable built results and a high-quality public realm by using physical form (rather than separation of uses) as the organizing principle for the code."[38]

The form-based code concept is presented in a book: *Form Based Codes: A Guide for Planners, Urban Designers, Municipalities, and Developers.*[39] In 2001, Carol Wyant coined the term *Form-Based Coding.* I have no idea what the term means, but I assume it is a catchword like Vonage, Skype, or Ooma.

In 2004, backers of the form-based code came together at a conference and consolidated their individual endeavors under a single brand name, The Form-Based Code Institute. The institute now speaks for many architects, urban designers, and planners who sell planning and design services to local government.

Backers of the form-based code claim it replaces Euclidian zoning, but in practice, form-based codes are what the State of California calls specific plans. Specific plans are plans that provide a substantial amount of detail.

SPECIFIC PLAN LAW

(a) A specific plan shall include a text and a diagram or diagrams which specify all of the following in detail:

(1) The distribution, location, and extent of the uses of land, including open space, within the area covered by the plan.

(2) The proposed distribution, location, and extent and intensity of major components of public and private transportation, sewage, water, drainage, solid waste disposal, energy, and other essential facilities proposed to be located within the area covered by the plan and needed to support the land uses described in the plan.

(3) Standards and criteria by which development will

proceed, and standards for the conservation, development, and utilization of natural resources, where applicable.

(4) A program of implementation measures including regulations, programs, public works projects, and financing measures necessary to carry out paragraphs (1), (2), and (3).

(b) The specific plan shall include a statement of the relationship of the specific plan to the general plan.

§65452. The specific plan may address any other subjects which in the judgment of the planning agency are necessary or desirable for implementation of the general plan." [40]

A MARKETING TOOL

The form-based code is a marketing tool, not a replacement for Euclidian zoning or its offshoots, incentive zoning and performance zoning.

A form-based code generally addresses the following issues:[41]

- A glossary of the precise use of terms;
- A project application and review process;
- A plan showing where different building form standards apply;
- Specifications for sidewalks, street lighting, on-street parking, travel lanes, street trees, street furniture, etc.; and
- Regulations that control the configuration, features, and functions of buildings.

A form-based code may also address the following supplementary issues:

- Regulations that control external architectural materials and quality;
- Regulations that control landscape design and plant materials, parking lot screening, street corner sight lines, pedestrian movements, etc.;

- Regulations that control sign dimensions, materials, illumination, and placement; and
- Regulations that control storm water drainage and infiltration, hillside development, tree protection, solar access, etc.

BOTH WORK WELL

I first used the California Specific Plan Law in the 1970s, while working as a redevelopment official. The redevelopment agency adopted a detailed specific plan for each project area, then invited property owners to redevelop their properties to comply with the project area's specific plan regulations and standards. If a proposed project complied with a plan's regulations and standards, all that a property owner had to do to rebuild or remodel was apply for a building permit, bypassing the jurisdiction's lengthy planning permit process.

Quick turnaround led to delightfully successful redevelopment. And the redevelopment agency got the type of development it wanted, a Mediterranean look and feel that enhanced the town's brand.

Based on my own experience, I can say that the form-based code should work extremely well in many situations; it just isn't zoning—it's planning.

Chapter 4
THE CODE OF ORDINANCES

When city hall wants to adopt a new land use regulation, the proposal goes through a legal process that requires review by staff, a public hearing before the planning commission acting as an advisory body, then a second public hearing before the city council acting as a decision-making body.

But, to complicate things for everyone, some jurisdictions think they can save time and effort by combining several unrelated items into a single ordinance:

- Section 1. RESIDENTIAL SWAMPLAND
- Section 2. BIG BOX BLOAT
- Section 3. COUNCIL QUORUM

After passing a three-item ordinance, the city clerk sends the newly passed ordinance to one of several national companies that code ordinances. Then the coding company strips away the peripheral material, such as the preamble, signatures, and vote tally, isolates the three items, and places each of them into a book arranged by subject matter. The book is called the code of ordinances. It contains all of the jurisdiction's regulations sorted into an accessible format.

There is no right or wrong way to compile a local code of ordinances. Each coding company uses a different technique. The table below shows two ways to code the same content. Either treatment is correct.

CODE OF ORDINANCES OPTIONS	
Coded by Company A	Coded by Company B
Title 1. RESIDENTIAL SWAMPLAND	Title 1. BIG BOX BLOAT
Title 2. COUNCIL QUORUM	Title 2. Land divisions
Title 3. Zoning	Title 3. Environment
Title 4. Subdivisions	Title 4. RESIDENTIAL SWAMPLAND
Title 5. Environmental protection	Title 5. Zoning districts
Title 6. BIG BOX BLOAT	Title 6. COUNCIL QUORUM

FILING SYSTEM

All you need to remember is that the ordinances themselves are the legal matter; the coding is nothing more than a convenient filing system. It is strictly up to the person who does the coding to determine how items will be divided. The goal is to make regulations easy to find, even if they don't make much sense.

YELLOW PAGES

The best analogy I can offer is the telephone directory yellow pages, where ads are sorted into categories describing the goods or services offered, rather than by the names or addresses of the stores. Just like the yellow pages, a well-crafted code of ordinances can save you a great deal of time finding what you are looking for.

INTERNAL CONSISTENCY

Because the code of ordinances is a filing system, there should not be any internal contradiction or inconsistence. If one part of the code of ordinances says "all public meetings start at 7 p.m.," another part of the code should not say "planning commission meetings start at 8 p.m." The code of ordinances must always be internally consistent and logical. If ordinances contradict each other, they are supposed to be reconciled before city hall passes them. But in the real world, of course, codes of ordinances often end up having severe contradictions. In practice, ordinances written years apart often contradict each other and new ordinances often repeat existing items already located in another title or chapter and long forgotten.

The important thing to remember is that the code of ordinances is only a filing system, and as such, should be arranged in the most convenient order without interfering with legal intent.

Chapter 5
COMBINING PERMIT REGULATIONS

The local code of ordinances is customarily divided into titles and chapters. Titles are the major headings, and chapters are minor headings. A code of ordinances may list all matters relating to revenue in one title, animal control in another title, and planning in a third title. But things can go terribly wrong and get badly mixed up.

CHICKEN OR EGG LEGISLATION

There is disagreement over whether subdivision or zoning came into existence first. The confusion exists because the federal government enacted zoning legislation two years before enacting planning and subdivision legislation.

STANDARD STATE ZONING ENABLING ACT OF 1926

This federal act was a model law states could follow in writing their own zoning regulations.

STANDARD CITY PLANNING ENABLING ACT OF 1928

This federal act was a model law that, among other things, addressed the control of private subdivision of land. But, of course, the historical record indicates subdivision goes back to the beginning of cities: "Between 5,000 and 3,000 B.C., prior to the invention of writing, real estate closings in Mesopotamia were conducted in front of a large number of witnesses."[42]

My first planning job was in a country that still used Mesopotamian-like property deeds. It was also a country with "a long history of military rule, corruption, poverty and crime—it is notorious for having the world's highest murder rate per capita."[43]

The country did not record deeds, and property owners had to fend for themselves, either by entrusting their documents to a lawyer, locking them in a safe deposit box, or hiding them under the mattress; the mattress was probably the safest.

While I was working in the country, I witnessed two incidents that taught me the importance of recording deeds with the county recorder's office. In the first incident, a real estate developer claimed ownership of a large parcel of land that was locally regarded to be communal farmland shared by six families. After a violent confrontation between the opponents, I was called in to mediate. But unknown to me, the developer had paid the local military leader to settle the dispute. By the time I arrived, my involvement had been reduced to disposing of six bodies. In the second incident, a real estate developer claimed title to a campesino's farm. When the developer showed up with deed in hand to claim his land, the campesino beheaded him and stuck his head on a fence post. The campesino said to me, "Now he can enjoy looking at my land forever."

LESSONS LEARNED: LAND USE REGULATIONS PROTECT RIGHTS

Land use regulations establish and protect your property rights. They also protect you from property owners who would damage the value of your property by creating a nuisance in a manner that would damage the quiet enjoyment of your property.

Another incident, this time in an old west mining town, taught me the need for accurate land surveying. I went out to an applicant's lot and found that the 1850s rod and chain surveying had created a paper lot that didn't exist on the land. The supposed property owner had bought a phantom lot. Fortunately, title insurance came to the rescue. Otherwise, I suppose, he would have had to cut off a neighbor's head.

EVOLVING LAND USE REGULATION

Once in a while a new type of regulation comes along that doesn't quite fit into the way the local code of ordinances is set up. When zoning came along in the early 1900s, most jurisdictions created a zoning title to add to their existing code of ordinances, even though there was probably a preexisting Mesopotamian-style subdivision title.

The quick fix created a Standard State Zoning Enabling Act of 1926 zoning title and a Standard City Planning Enabling Act of 1928 subdivision title. Creating a new zoning title looked good at the time but proved to be a serious blunder in the long run, as I will make clear to you as we move along.

TITLE AND CHAPTER ARRANGEMENT

Generally, a local code of ordinances has between 15 and 30 titles, and the names of the titles will differ from code to code. The subject matter in each title will also be slightly different from code to code but generally recognizable.

There is no universal agreement as to how the titles should be arranged. In one code, subdivision will be listed as Title 11 and zoning will be listed as Title 12. In another code, subdivision may be listed as Title 17 and zoning listed as Title 20. It doesn't make any difference in which order the subject matter is presented in the code of ordinances. What is important is that the material be presented in the most useful and logical way.

Within each title, the chapters are also arranged arbitrarily. Once again, all that matters is that the material be presented so you can find it.

The number and length of titles are not fixed or standardized. They can be long or short, lumped together or split apart. There is no reason why one title cannot be divided into two titles or four titles or six titles. From a legal standpoint, it makes no difference whatsoever; it's just a matter of style. Just remember, ordinances are coded only for convenience; they can be coded in any way that makes sense.

ONE SIMPLE ERROR

Now that I've told you a code can be constructed any old way, let me tell you about the one simple coding error that has caused untold grief: dividing subdivision and zoning titles.

Subdivision and zoning titles should have been combined into a single title, right from the start. Subdivision and zoning should never have been placed in the code of ordinances as separate, unrelated titles.

COMBINING SUBDIVISION AND ZONING

To give you an idea of the direction I'm headed, I'm starting this explanation with a series of tables that show the way codes of ordinances have typically dealt with zoning and subdivision and demonstrate how the existing way can be changed into a simpler and more useful approach.

What I did was start out with the standard way subdivision and zoning appear in most codes of ordinances, then I combined subdivision and zoning into a single title. Through research and testing, I found that combining subdivision and zoning solves all sorts of long-standing problems planners have come up against in processing planning permits.

SEPARATE CODE TITLES

The two following tables show what it looks like when subdivision and zoning are coded as two separate titles.

Title 20–Subdivision		
Ch 1: General Provisions	Ch 5: Final Map	Ch 9: Preliminary Soil Report
Ch 2: Definitions	Ch 6: Parcel Map	Ch 10: Certificate of Compliance
Ch 3: Standards	Ch 7: Other Maps	Ch 11: Condominium Conversion
Ch 4: Tentative Map	Ch 8: Exception	Ch 12: Merger of Parcels

Title 21–Zoning		
Ch 1: Zoning Plan	Ch 8: Industrial District	Ch 15: Enforcement
Ch 2: Zone Districts	Ch 9: Planned Development	Ch 16: Home Occupations
Ch 3: R-1 Residential District	Ch 10: General Provisions	Ch 17: Signs
Ch 4: R-2 Residential District	Ch 11: Nonconforming Use	Ch 18: Off-Street Parking
Ch 5: R-3 Residential District	Ch 12: Variance	Ch 19: Mobile Homes
Ch 6: Commercial District	Ch 13: Amendments	Ch 20: Design Review
Ch 7: Definitions	Ch 14: Appeal	Ch 21: Zone Boundaries

You've probably seen this arrangement or something close to it. It is an arrangement I am determined to change. What I want to get across to you is the understanding that subdivision and zoning are listed in this way purely by historical accident.

In researching this topic, I found there is absolutely no advantage to separating subdivision and zoning into two separate titles, so I asked myself what would happen if I shuffled the subdivision and zoning titles together into one title and them listed them in the code of ordinances as a single title.

RANDOMLY MIXED TITLES

The following table shows what happens when I mix the two titles together.

Subdivision and Zoning Titles Intermixed		
Ch 13: Amendments	Ch 14: Appeal	Ch 10: Certificate of Compliance
Ch 6: Commercial District	Ch 11: Condominium Conversion	Ch 2: Definitions
Ch 7: Definitions	Ch 20: Design Review	Ch 15: Enforcement
Ch 8: Exception	Ch 5: Final Map	Ch 1: General Provisions
Ch 10: General Provisions	Ch 16: Home Occupations	Ch 8: Industrial District
Ch 12: Merger of Parcels	Ch 19: Mobile Homes	Ch 11: Nonconforming Use
Ch 18: Off-Street Parking	Ch 7: Other Maps	Ch 6: Parcel Map
Ch 9: Planned Development	Ch 9: Preliminary Soil Report	Ch 3: R-1 Residential District
Ch 4: R-2 Residential District	Ch 5: R-3 Residential District	Ch 17: Signs
Ch 3: Standards	Ch 4: Tentative Map	Ch 12: Variance
Ch 21: Zone Boundaries	Ch 2: Zone Districts	Ch 1: Zoning Plan

NOTHING HAPPENS

When I combine the two titles together, it turns out that nothing happens. Mixing the two titles together didn't change anything, so I figured that maybe there was no reason why there should have been two separate titles in the first place.

What caught my attention was that the only reason subdivision and zoning are often presented as two separate titles is because they came into existence at different times. Had they been created at the same point in time, they would have been lumped together as a single title right from the start.

SHUFFLING THE DECK

When I combined the two titles into one title composed of thirty chapters, I found that the thirty chapters had a pattern to them. So, I again sorted and shuffled them into groups that made more sense. I eventually found I was able to shuffle the thirty-chapter deck down to four suits: (procedures-black ♠), (permits-red ♥), (districts-green ♦), and (standards-yellow ♣). I figured four suits would be a lot easier to play with than a thirty-chapter deck.

I found that every scrap of information in the thirty subdivision and zoning chapters fit neatly into one of the four suits, with nothing left over and nothing left out. It was a perfect fit.

Once I understood the logic of the four titles, I found I could never go back to the pointless two title tradition.

It may not yet seem important to you, but changing the way the code is structured makes all the difference in the world when it comes to processing permits. It is a fundamental breakthrough.

Subdivision and Zoning Sorted by Suit	
Procedures-♠	Permits-♥
Ch 2: Definitions	Ch 14: Appeal
Ch 7: Definitions	Ch 13: Amendments
Ch 15: Enforcement	Ch 10: Certificate of Compliance
Ch 1: General Provisions	Ch 11: Condominium Conversion
Ch 10: General Provisions	Ch 20: Design Review
Ch 21: Zone Boundaries	Ch 8: Exception
Ch 2: Zone Districts	Ch 5: Final Map
Ch 1: Zoning Plan	Ch 16: Home Occupation
	Ch 12: Merger of Parcels
	Ch 7: Other Maps
	Ch 6: Parcel Map
	Ch 9: Planned Development
	Ch 4: Tentative Map
	Ch 12: Variance
Districts-♦	Standards-♣
Ch 3: R-1 Residential	Ch 3: Standards
Ch 4: R-2 Residential	Ch 18: Off-Street Parking
Ch 5: R-3 Residential	Ch 19: Mobile Homes
Ch 6: Commercial	Ch 9: Preliminary Soil Report
Ch 8: Industrial	Ch 17: Signs
	Ch 11: Nonconforming Use

Merely by combining subdivision and zoning into one unified title and then splitting it into four suits, I've eliminated all of the inherent conflicts caused by the tradition of arbitrarily dividing land use into subdivision and zoning.

A COMMON SENSE SYSTEM

Suddenly I had a system that made sense. I had created a single land use title divided into four suits that could be keyed into a computer and programmed to produce an automated planning department, something the hopelessly illogical subdivision and zoning titles always defied.

My next job was to make sure the four new code suits were complete and accurate, because computers are single-minded demons that don't do well guessing what you have on your mind.

My next quest was to see if anything was missing. If something was missing, I needed to find it and make sure it would fit into one of the four suits. I knew that if I found just one item that didn't fit into one of the four suits, all my previous effort would be lost in failure. Just as a physicist feels the need to add up all the visible matter and dark matter, I felt a need to add up all the known land use matter and unknown land use matter.

Right off the bat, I found that a lot of important land use matter was missing from the equation, information my unforgiving computer would demand to have if it was going to take over the routine work I hate to do by hand.

Chapter 6
LOOKING AT PROCEDURES

There are two ways to approach procedures:
- Listing the authority and duties of the city council, planning commission, zoning board of adjustment, and planning staff.
- Listing the planning permit processing options.

AUTHORITY AND DUTIES

Nance County, Nebraska, lists the authority and duties of public officials:

> The purpose of the Planning and Zoning Procedures is to assist Nance County in the implementation of the Comprehensive Plan, Zoning Regulations, and Subdivision Regulations. The County Board of Supervisors, Planning Commission, Zoning Administrator, and the Zoning Board of Adjustment are responsible for the enforcement of the plan and its implementation through utilization of the Zoning Regulations and Subdivision Regulations.[44]

PROCESSING OPTIONS

I prefer to reduce the list of authority and duties to the bare minimum legal requirements and move them closer to the beginning of the jurisdiction's code of ordinances, listing them under Title 1– GENERAL PROVISIONS or some other part of the code of ordinances, such as "regulations, procedures, and bylaws," that deals with organizational housekeeping.

PERMIT PROCESSING PROCEDURES

At about the same time jurisdictions started issuing planning permits, back near the beginning of the twentieth century, the courts started ruling on the legality and applicability of the new zoning concepts coming into play across the country.

But rather than address planning permits themselves, the courts addressed permit processing procedures. The legal system was concerned about the fairness of zoning and wanted to make sure zoning was on the up-and-up and did not deprive the general public of their property rights.

Early on, the courts started addressing zoning issues in terms of three legal categories: legislative, adjudicative, and ministerial. Over the years, state laws and court cases have suggested that all planning permits fit into one of these three categories. The courts also shied away from ad-hoc categories of permits, such as the ones many jurisdictions call "land use entitlements."

Based on the accumulation of court opinions, you can be assured that you don't need an open-ended list of processes that go on and on forever; You can safely assign every planning permit to just one of three categories: legislative, adjudicative, or ministerial.

In case law, the three terms appear over and over again. On the other hand, the three terms are almost never mentioned in land use regulations. It's as if planners and lawyers work with completely different subject matter with no common ground whatsoever.

LEGISLATIVE ACTION

A legislative action is the exercise of the power to make rules by a body empowered to do so. There is no inherent concept of right or wrong in legislative action. That's about as close as I can get to it. A legislative act can be anything from beneficial to ruinous. Governing bodies like to think they enact appropriate and beneficial legislation, but they are often misled by a lack of critical thinking or their inability to make clear, reasoned judgments.

ADJUDICATIVE ACTION

An adjudicative or quasi-judicial action is an action that is subject to judgment. The adjudicative process is governed by rules of evidence and procedure. Its objective is to reach a reasonable settlement of the application for a planning permit. An impartial, passive fact finder, usually called the planning commission, renders the decision. The planning commission must establish the facts and define and interpret the applicable laws.

MINISTERIAL ACTION

A ministerial action is performed in accordance with law and established procedures without exercising any individual judgment or discretion. In judging a planning permit, the law does not allow for judgment or variation.

SIMPLE AND EFFECTIVE PROCEDURES

By relegating authority and duties to Title 1 - GENERAL PROVISIONS or some other part of the code of ordinances that deals with organizational housekeeping, planning permit processing is left unburdened by non–land use issues. This frees up the procedures chapter to concentrate on the all-important legislative, adjudicative, and ministerial permit processes.

MISSING PROCEDURES?

So, what about those missing procedures? It turned out that there were far too many procedures and too many of the wrong kind of procedures. So, my task ended up being one of weeding out procedures that cluttered up the code of ordinances and detracted from my goal of uncovering common sense zoning.

Chapter 7
LOOKING AT PERMITS

The first thing I did when I started looking at permits was to look at the commonly used generic subdivision and zoning regulations. I was disappointed to find that the generic regulations listed only twelve permits, including one item, "Home Occupation," that is not even a planning permit.

Generic Zoning and Subdivision Planning Permits	
Ch 13: Amendments	Ch 16: Home Occupation
Ch 10: Certificate of Compliance	Ch 7: Other Maps
Ch 11: Condominium Conversion	Ch 6: Parcel Map
Ch 20: Design Review	Ch 9: Planned Development
Ch 8: Exception	Ch 4: Tentative Map
Ch 5: Final Map	Ch 12: Variance

After finding so few permits listed in the most commonly used set of land use regulations, I decided to look further, so I went on the internet and found three more lists of planning permits—all from similar cities within a single state. To my surprise, what I found were three distinctively different planning permit listings:

- City A listed thirteen planning permits.
- City B listed nineteen planning permits.
- City C listed eleven planning permits.

The disparity between the three jurisdictions left me perplexed; how could there be such a divergence? The only planning permit all three had in common was the variance.

I have always assumed that jurisdictions from coast to coast would list the same planning permits in their regulations. How could it be otherwise?

Planning Permits, Three City Comparison		
City A	City B	City C
Design Review	Annexation	Rezoning/Planned Unit Development Permit
General Plan Amendment	Appeals	Short Term Rental Permit (Coastal Zone)
Heritage Tree Removal Permit	Certificate of Substantial Conformance	Street Name Change Permit
Lot Line Adjustments/ Mergers	Conditional Use Permit (CUP)	Temporary Event Permit
Non-conforming Exception Permit	Environmental Review	Timberland Preserve Zone Permit
Preliminary and Precise Development Plan	General Plan Amendment	Tree Trimming and Removal Permit
Rezoning and Zoning Ordinance Amendments	Home Occupation Permit	Use Permit for Child Care Facilities
Second Dwelling Units	Lot Merger	Use Permits for Telecommunications Facilities
Sign Permit	Lot Line Adjustment	Use Permit
Slope Use Permit	Minor Subdivision (Parcel Map)	Variance
Subdivision	Rezoning (Zoning Text or Map Amendment)	Williamson Act
Use Permit	Second Unit Permit	
Variance	Setback Adjustments and Temporary Uses	
	Site Development Permit (Plot Plan)	
	Specific Plan/Specific Plan Amendment	
	Standard Subdivision (Tentative Tract Map)	
	Temporary Event Permit	
	Time Extension	
	Variance	

EXPANDED PERMIT SEARCH

After my surprise finding, I went on a reading binge, looking at over 200 sets of land use regulations—a wide variation did indeed exist.

But I intuitively knew that the list of planning permits had to be uniform from coast to coast, because land use regulations all stem from similar state zoning enabling acts and are all subject to the same court rulings. So why was I coming across so much diversity and so little uniformity?

STUCK WITH IMPOSSIBILITY

Eventually I had to accept without proof that many planning permits just don't get written down in land use regulations, even though they are known to exist and are issued by jurisdictions all across the country. I also had to accept the fact that jurisdictions hide well-known permits by giving them local slang names—names that may be quaint and colorful but also somewhat confusing to the general public.

Anyone who has worked in a planning department for any time at all knows that over the years, some thoroughly legitimate planning permits get lumped together as "amendments" or "other maps," instead of being listed by their formal names. Lumping planning permits together confuses people who may need to know exactly what planning permits are issued by city hall. A generic term such as "amendment" might refer to a general plan amendment, a zoning map amendment, a subdivision map amendment, or one of several other amendments. And "other maps" could mean a lot line adjustment, a merger of parcels, or a reversion to acreage. Offhand language can lead to confusion and misunderstanding.

Other planning permits are even more obscure, such as the environmental impact statement (EIS), environmental assessment (EA), and coastal management permits. Most often, a poorly understood process, like a negative declaration or initial study, ends up being tagged onto the end of a staff report written for some more traditional planning permit, such as a conditional use permit (CUP).

If you read a few codes of ordinances, court cases, and journal articles, you will find that local planners have come up with pet names for their favorite permits.

Planning Permit Names	
Slang Name	Proper Name
Minor Subdivision	Partition
Major Subdivision	Subdivision
Lot Split	Partition
Rezone	Zoning Ordinance Amendment
Minor Use	Temporary Use Permit*
Major Use	Conditional Use Permit
Not a legitimate planning permit. It is a business license.	

PERIODIC TABLE OF PERMITS

In due course, I found an analogy that I think may explain the missing permit conundrum. Try to think of missing permits this way: Science uses a chart called the periodic table of elements. The table is a list of elements numbered one through 118.

Up until recently, science had only found 112 elements out of the 118. But as of 2016, elements 113, 115, 117, and 118 have also been discovered and officially confirmed by the International Union of Pure and Applied Chemistry.[45]

Just like the periodic table of elements, planners know there ought to be a lot more planning permits than the twenty listed in the generic land use regulations, because they are discussed in court findings, named in state law, and recounted in the oral tradition when planners gather around the campfire after a hard day's work.

So far, I have found about fifteen or more missing or unknown planning permits to add to the original list of twelve or so planning permits. For all that I know, the periodic table of permits may go as high as fifty, if you allow for all the ones that could just pop out of the space-time continuum. I like to think that looking for missing planning permits is like going on a cosmic Easter egg hunt.

THE CONCEPT OF COVENANTS

In law, a covenant is a promise written into a deed conveying real property: "A covenant running with the land (real covenant) is a promise that can be enforced by the successors to the original covenantee and against the successors to the original covenantor. Its benefits or burdens run automatically without the need for an assignment of rights or delegation of duties."[46]

A planning permit is a promise written into a deed. A planning permit runs with the land and cannot be separated from the land, nor can the land be transferred without transferring the planning permit.

When looking for missing planning permits, the first thing I do is make sure the item runs with the land. Is it a promise written into a deed?

MISSING OR MISLEADING

In my search for missing planning permits, I've eliminated quite a few misleading items that are not planning permits at all—temporary event permits, setback adjustments, temporary uses, tree trimming and removal permits, and home occupations.

The following list is composed of items I consider to be legitimate planning permits based on my understanding of laws and court rulings. The list is not complete—it is expandable to include other items a jurisdiction may need to include to meet its specific needs.

Remember, there are only three categories of planning permits: legislative, adjudicative, and ministerial. The subcategories I list (ANX, CUP, VAR) are well-known common names people use when talking about planning permits. They are the common names of the application forms and other paperwork and are used for convenience only.

PLANNING PERMISSION INCLUDING COMMON NAMES

Legislative Planning Permits-♥

(ANX) Annexation (Change of Organization)

    (ANP) Annexation—Preliminary

    (ANL) LAFCO (Local Agency Formation Commission)
        Processing Annexation

    (ANF) Annexation—Final

(DEV) Development Agreement

(FBC) Form-based Code

(GPA) General Plan Adoption or Amendment

    (GPM) General Plan Map Adoption or Amendment

    (GPT) General Plan Text Adoption or Amendment

(LCP) Local Coastal Program Adoption or Amendment

(PDZ) Planned Development Zoning

(PRZ) Prezone of Unincorporated Territory

(SPA) Specific Plan Adoption or Amendment

(ZOA) Zoning Ordinance Adoption or Amendment

    (ZMA) Zoning Map Adoption or Amendment

    (ZTA) Zoning Text Adoption or Amendment

Adjudicative Planning Permits-♥

(CDP) Coastal Development Proposal

(CND) Condominium Conversion

(CUP) Conditional Use Permit

(EIS) Environmental Impact Statement

    (aka Environmental Impact Report or EIR)

(PDP) Planned Development Proposal

(LLA) Lot Line Adjustment

(PNP) Partition Proposal (aka Tentative Parcel Map or TPM)

(RTA) Reversion to Acreage

(SDR) Site Design Review

(SPX) Subdivision Proposal Exception

(SUB) Subdivision Proposal (aka Tentative Subdivision Map or TSM)

(VAR) Variance

Ministerial Planning Permits–♥

(BLD) Building Permit

(COC) Certificate of Compliance

(COO) Certificate of Occupancy

(ENV) Environmental Assessment (aka Initial Study)

(PTP) Partition Plat (aka Final Parcel Map or FPM)

(SDP) Subdivision Plat (aka Final Subdivision Map or FSM)

(MOP) Merger of Parcels

(PTE) Permit Time Extension

(TME) Subdivision Time Extension

(VRE) Vesting Rights Time Extension

OPEN-ENDED AND EXPANDABLE

The list of common planning permit names (ANX, CUP, VAR, etc.) is open-ended and can expand to meet any contingency. It would not be at all unreasonable for city hall to list forty or more common planning permit names.

I already know you are going to ask why we should separate the zoning text amendment from the zoning map amendment; why not do it the usual way and just call it a rezone? Well, there is an excellent reason for not calling it a rezone. Using a common name, such as rezone, worked just fine before planning offices started using computers. But now, when virtually every planner processes permits on a computer, planners find they can use computer programs to take the handwork out of permit processing. With programming, it is possible to create forms, reports, and public notices precisely tailored to each type of planning permit application. In this case, a zoning text amendment (ZTA) requires a different public notification process than does a zoning map amendment (ZMA). If you don't separate the two, the computer program won't know which public notice process applies to the situation.

By simply differentiating between a zoning text amendment (ZTA) and zoning map amendment (ZMA), a computer subroutine can be written that prints out only the correct notification documents. (Yes, I've found that the jurisdiction can charge for two separate permit applications if the proposal changes both text and map. Some jurisdictions limit submission of zoning text amendment applications to four specific months during the year—Jan., Apr., Jul., Oct.)

COMPUTERIZATION

Computerization can save a great deal of time, but it requires exacting use of the language, because computers can't make interpretations; they just do what they are told to do—nothing more, nothing less—like most people.

After creating my list of planning permits, I set about eliminating current planning as we know it. I wrote a set of internal procedures and forms that standardize the work that goes on in the planning office by eliminating inefficient processes and the overload of paperwork.

CONFUSING PERMIT NAMES

Some planning permit names confuse the public and need to be changed. Other wording appears to have been deliberately placed into state laws just to confuse the general public.

The following confusing terminology is used by states: *preliminary* and *tentative*. The terms, I suspect, were introduced into state law by devious persons who knew they would work against fair dealing and honest government.

Any educated person knows that:

• preliminary means introductory or preparatory; and

• tentative means unsure, uncertain, or hesitant.

But in California, a Tentative Parcel Map or Tentative Subdivision Map grants permission to grade the land, install infrastructure, and create finished lots ready for building. There is nothing unsure, uncertain, or hesitant about it.

Some states (Pennsylvania and Virginia) use the equally confusing term *preliminary subdivision plan*. Below is an online conversation between me and a city clerk in Pennsylvania:

My Inquiry: "I am looking for the administrative record for the Vineyard Commons project."

Township Response (verbatim from an email): "Vineyard Commons is a PRELIMINARY land development application. It is too early for any permits; this is only the first step in the process. They will have to come back with a FINAL plan submission and go thru the process again for final."[47]

In actuality, the "PRELIMINARY" land development application granted permission to regrade the land; install drainage and sanitary sewers; install streetlights; construct curbs, gutters, and streets; and subdivide the land into small finished lots ready to sell.

By using the term "PRELIMINARY," the town led the public to believe there would be another public hearing where they could continue to voice their opposition to the subdivision.

Even the misinformed and befuddled township leaders thought there would be another public hearing—but it was all over but the crying.

Chapter 8
LOOKING AT DISTRICTS

♦

I'm going to show you what I found when I went out looking for zoning districts in codes of ordinances from randomly chosen jurisdictions.

ZONING DISTRICTS

When I started looking, I had no idea how many zoning districts I would find in run-of-the-mill codes of ordinances. I found a lot more than I thought I would—certainly far more than necessary or desirable.

Zoning Districts		
R-1 Single-Family Residential	C-1 Neighborhood Commercial	M-1 Light Industrial
R-2 Duplex Residential	C-2 General Commercial	M-2 Medium Industrial
R-3 Multiple-Family Residential	C-3 Highway Commercial	M-3 Heavy Industrial
R-4 Multiple-Family Low-Rise	C-4 Historic Commercial	M-4 Specialty Industrial
R-5 Multiple-Family Mid-Rise	C-5 Super-Regional Center	M-5 Fabricating Processing
R-6 Multiple-Family High-Rise	C-M Commercial Industrial	P-I Planned Industrial
F-P Flood Plain	P-C Planned Commercial	

Instead of looking for missing zoning districts, I ended up trying to figure out how to get rid of excessive zoning districts.

REDUNDANT ZONING DISTRICTS

Many codes of ordinances, especially those for big cities, list obsolete or redundant zoning districts. They end up with zoning maps that look as if every lot has its own zoning district. Most of these excessive zoning districts appear to be left over from many decades ago, when zoning was thought to be a cure-all for the ills of society.

CURE-ALL ZONING

I was recently involved in a case where an applicant applied for a Zoning Map Amendment (ZMA) in the city of Phoenix, Arizona. The applicant wanted to convert an existing (P-1) Limited Passenger Automobile Parking lot to an (R-5 H-R) Multifamily Residence District, High-Rise and High-Density apartment building.

The proposal would have replaced the surface parking lot with a 164-foot-tall, 15-story multifamily residential building—just a minor change.

The neighborhood association took the position that the proposal constituted unwarranted spot zoning. In reviewing the case, I was surprised to find that Phoenix has sixty-six zoning districts; it is a city of spot zoning. One citizen comment said, "Spot zoning—isn't that illegal?"

Phoenix has quaint old regulations—they appear to date from the 1930s or the 1950s. Phoenix may have more zoning districts than any other city in the world.

Having sixty-six zoning districts could easily lead to spot zoning—in fact, the zoning map indicates that spot zoning is common all over Phoenix. Phoenix is a hodgepodge of poorly situated sprawl.

Phoenix Zoning Districts	
Suburban S-1 District-Ranch or Farm Residence	Planned Community (PC) District
Suburban S-2 District-Ranch or Farm Commercial	Planned Shopping Center (PSC) District
Residential Estate RE-43 District-One-Family Residence	Regional Shopping Center (RSC) District
Residential Estate RE-24 District-One-Family Residence	Parking P-1 District-Passenger Automobile Parking
Residential R1-14 District-One-Family Residence	P-2 Parking
RE-35 Single-Family Residence District	Golf Course (GC) District
R1-18 Single-Family Residence District	Urban Residential (UR) District
R1-10 Single-Family Residence District	Airport Noise Impact Overlay (AIO) District
R1-8 Single-Family Residence District	Capitol Mall Overlay District
R1-6 Single-Family Residence District	Special Permit Uses
R-2 Multifamily Residence District	Uses Not Permitted Within Corporate Limits
R-3 Multifamily Residence District	Mixed Use Agricultural (MUA) District
R-3A Multifamily Residence District	The Historic Canal-Side Restaurant Overlay District
R-4 Multifamily Residence District	Baseline Area Overlay District
R-5 Multifamily Residence District	Arcadia Camelback Special Planning
R-4A District-Multifamily Residence-General	Desert Character Overlay Districts
R-O District-Restricted Commercial	North Black Canyon Overlay District
Residential Office R-O District-Restricted Commercial	Rio Salado Interim Overlay (RSIO) District
Commercial Office C-O District-Restricted Commercial	Central City South Interim Overlay (CCSIO) District
Commercial C-1	Section 657. FH-Flood Hazard and Erosion Management District
Commercial C-2 District-Intermediate Commercial	Deer Valley Airport Overlay (DVAO) District
Commercial C-3 District-General Commercial	Planned Shopping Center Overlay District
B3-Special Commercial	Four Corners Overlay District

Phoenix Zoning Districts	
Commerce Park District	South Phoenix Village and Target Area B Design Overlay
A-1 Light Industrial District	Interim Transit-Oriented Zoning Overlay District One (TOD-1)
A-2 Industrial District	Interim Transit-Oriented Zoning Overlay District Two (TOD-2)
RH Resort District	North Central Avenue Special Planning District (SPD) Overlay District
Residential Infill R-I District-Multifamily Residential	Seventh Avenue Urban Main Street Overlay (SAUMSO) District
High-Rise H-R District-High-Rise and High-Density District	East Buckeye Road Overlay (EBRO) District
High-Rise H-R1 District-High-Rise and High-Density District	Summary List of Special Planning and Specific Plan Overlay Districts
High-Rise Incentive District-High-Rise and Mixed-Use District	Arts, Culture and Small Business Overlay (ACOD) District
Mid-Rise District	Planned Unit Development (PUD)
Planned Area Development	Hatcher Road Overlay (HRO) District

I have no idea why any jurisdiction would want to have so many zoning districts—what's the point of it?

BASIC ZONING

Below is a suggested way city hall could reduce the number of zoning districts to a minimum. However, I would expect most jurisdictions would want to have a few more districts.

Zoning Districts—♦	
(AR) Acreage Residential	(NC) Neighborhood Commercial
(LR) Low-Density Residential	(GC) General Commercial
(MR) Medium-Density Residential	(LI) Light Industrial
(HR) High-Density Residential	(HI) Heavy Industrial

By cutting the number of zoning districts to eight, a jurisdiction could greatly simplify planning permit complexity without sacrificing zoning safeguards. In some situations, a jurisdiction may need to add more zoning districts to cover special circumstances such as: Historic

Town Center (HC) or Beach Front Residential (BR). Houston, Texas, might want to have a Riverbed Residential District (RR) or perhaps a "floating" zone.

OVERLAY DISTRICTS

Another way to reduce zoning districts, or to at least avoid some of the worst effects of excessive zoning districts, is to use overlay districts. An overlay district can be used to modify underlying zoning without creating a whole new zoning district. Overlay districts are useful in defining redevelopment project areas where the whole land mass can be blanketed with a redevelopment overlay district requiring a specific development strategy.

An overlay district is a designation superimposed on a parcel to modify or restrict land use without replacing or changing the parcel's zoning district designation.

Overlay Zoning Districts–♦	
(GWOD) Greenway Overlay	(PDOD) Planned Development Overlay
(REOD) Redevelopment Overlay	(FPOD) Flood Plain Overlay

Zoning need not be elaborate to be clear and effective. A jurisdiction could zone effectively with as few as eight zoning districts and four overlay districts.

CLASSIFICATION SYMBOLS

I hope you have been observant enough to notice that my system assigns orderly combinations of symbols:

- **Zoning districts**—AR, LR, LI
- **Planning permits**—CUP, ZTA, PUD, SUB
- **Overlay districts**—GWOD, REOD, PDOD, FDOD
- **Planning permit applications**—2019-ZMA-023, 2019-SUB-043, 2019-PUD-003

An orderly combination of symbols prevents errors and omissions from occurring in the planning office. It is also easier to memorize and remember than the scrambled mess Phoenix uses.

Chapter 9
LOOKING AT STANDARDS

The law refers to land use standards as objective criteria. Standards are rules that apply to physical properties such as minimum lot size, lot dimensions, side yard setback, or maximum building height.

A standard can be a simple statement: "A single-family dwelling must have at least 900 square feet of floor area." Or, a standard may be complex, such as the lengthy requirements for swimming pool safety:

No swimming pool is allowed in a front yard or a side yard. The minimum setback for a swimming pool is five (5) feet from rear lot line, five (5) feet from an interior side lot line, fifteen (15) feet from a street side lot line, and ten (10) feet from any building on the lot. A solid, noise dampening fence or wall, six (6) feet tall, must enclose the rear yard including the swimming pool to protect neighboring lots from excessive noise. A chain link fence not less than three-and-one-half (3½) feet tall, and not more than five (5) feet tall, may be installed close to the pool as a safety precaution. Any gate leading to the pool must be self-closing and self-latching. The latch must open only by key or combination lock. The pool enclosing fence must have no openings larger than four

(4) inches in any dimension. (The above sample has been reduced from much longer, more detailed federal standard.)

OBJECTIVITY

I once observed two groups of census takers. One group lived in a run-down, impoverished neighborhood, and the other group lived in an upscale gated community. When the two groups were asked to report on local housing conditions, the people from the poor neighborhood reported few dilapidated houses while the affluent group found most houses to be dilapidated.

In spot-checking both groups, I found that the affluent group considered any house with a weedy front lawn to be dilapidated while the impoverished group considered any barely habitable house to be sound.

Objective standards are not easy to write. They must be measurable in some way, such as by applying a rubric listing specific criterion for grading or scoring compliance.

Classroom teachers use scoring rubrics to grade assignments.

Homework Assignment Rubric					
Grade	A	B	C	D	F
Homework completed	100%	75%	50%	25%	0%

FINDING STANDARDS

Traditionally, standards have been scattered throughout land use regulations without regard for ease of use. It is often extremely difficult to find standards. In many land use regulations, standards are not set apart in their own section where they can be clearly seen. They are mixed into paragraphs that address other issues.

SHORTAGE OF STANDARDS

Another problem with the typical code is the shortage of standards. The code used as our example only lists twenty-three standards. But when I read through a lot of land use regulations looking for standards, I was able to find dozens more, many of which were intermixed with definitions procedures and other items. Wouldn't it be nice if someone placed standards in one single location called "Standards"?

The following table lists sixty-five standards I was able to glean from generic land use regulations used by many cities.

Standards (Including Hidden Standards)-♣		
Address Numbering	Agricultural Buffer	Alley
Antenna or Mast	Block Configuration	Building Height Limit
Building Setback	Cabaret or Tavern	Cemetery
Condo Conversion	Contractor Shack	Curb and Gutter
Day Care	Demolition	Disabled Access
Drainage	Dwelling, Guest	Dwelling, Secondary
Dwelling, Size	Dwelling, Temporary	Easement or Reservation
Energy Conservation	Expo or Concert	Fence or Wall
Flag Lot	Garage, Residential	Gas Station
Grading	Hazardous Substance	Lot Design
Mailboxes	Manufactured Homes	Meeting House
Mobile Homes	Monuments, Survey	Motor Vehicle Repair
Partition Plan or Map	Railroad Crossing	Residential Care Home
Satellite TV	School Site Dedication	Seasonal Sales
Service Roads	Sewer Service	Sidewalks
Sign Structure Design	Site Design	Soils Report, Preliminary
Street Design	Street Furniture	Streetlights
Street Names	Street Signs	Street Tree Protection
Subdivision, New	Subdivision Plan or Map	Swimming Pool
Tract Sales Office	Trash Bins	Trees
Underground Utilities	Vehicle Storage	Vision Clear Zone
Water Courses	Water Service	

If I looked a little harder, I could have easily found more hidden standards. You should be able to find at least sixty-five—it doesn't take much effort to root out missing standards.

CATEGORIES OF STANDARDS

Because there are so many standards, it is probably better to assign them to subcategories:

- Planning standards
- Improvement standards
- Aesthetic standards
- Safety standards

The standards in this book are informational only. You will need to transfer your own standards into the model.

Chapter 10
STACKING THE DECK

Stacking the deck means to fix something so a desired outcome is achieved. By stacking the deck, I was able to combine the two title format into a single title. Once I came to understand the logic behind the single title, four suit format, I found I could never go back to the pointless two titles and thirty-chapter traditional format.

A COMMON SENSE APPROACH

Suddenly I had a system that made sense. I had created four land use suits that were logical enough for a computer to deal with. This made it possible to key in data to produce an automated planning department, something the hopelessly illogical two-title, presentation always defied.

The rest of this book explains what I had to do to provide my computer with enough raw matter to satisfy its appetite.

INHERENT LIMITATIONS

As I worked toward completing my common sense Euclidian zoning regulations, I came to realize two truths: Euclidian zoning can't turn your community into a nice place to live, but common sense zoning can greatly reduce your workload and save you money.

So, the big reason to switch to common sense zoning is to save you a lot of time and money. It's not going to fix your community; for that, you will have to look elsewhere—perhaps to your local plans.

The other reason to switch to common sense zoning is to turn your mundane, routine planning job from stultifying drudgery to a relatively pleasant creative pastime. With more free time available, you can use your technical ability to write better staff reports and exercise your moral authority by dedicating effort toward improving the current state of local planning.

Zoning is static law that establishes allowable land use, lot size, density, height, and floor area ratio in systematic order. Planning is dynamic activity that decides in advance what to do, how to do it, and when to do it. Zoning preserves; planning creates.

Zoning is conservation directed; planning is goal directed. No amount of zoning will take a city from where it is to where it wants to be—only planning can do that.

Chapter 11
ACCORDING TO HOYLE

Edmond Hoyle (1672–1769) became famous for his writing about card game rules. The phrase "according to Hoyle" has come to mean an appeal to an accepted authority.[48] Codes of ordinances usually contain two types of game rules that can easily end up in the land use title, where they may confuse and disrupt.

GENERAL PROVISIONS

Every set of land use regulations I've ever read contains rules that are necessary for governing the jurisdiction but may confuse the reader or disrupt the flow of the text. These rules should never be written into the land use title.

Some firms that assemble codes of ordinances dispose of general rules at the beginning of the code of ordinances and refer to them as "General Provisions." This methodology seems to work quite well.

The following excerpt is an example of one of those rules that should be located where it will not interfere with the land use title:

3.101 - Planning Director.

The Planning Director shall carry out all responsibilities of the office of the Zoning Administrator as defined in Arizona Revised Statutes and set forth hereafter.[49]

IN-HOUSE PROCEDURES

Procedures used by staff in carrying out their duties need not be written down in the code of ordinances.

I found the following unnecessary information in the same local code of ordinances:

> Applications shall be filed with the Planning Department on an application form with the required documentation specified on guidelines provided by the Planning Director with appropriate fees.[50]

IN-HOUSE PROCEDURES MANUAL

No one outside of the planning department needs to know who does what. Instructions to staff should be kept in some sort of procedures manual. And they should be informal, easy to amend, and flexible. They should not be adopted as laws or regulations.

The land use regulations written into the code of ordinances should contain as little as possible because:

- they must be formally adopted;
- they are difficult and expensive to amend;
- they lock in in-house permit processing procedures; and
- they formalize casual relationships and ways of interacting.

The in-house procedures manual, like the personnel manual, is designed to address job responsibilities and ways of doing things—it needs to be flexible and informal.

COGNITIVE DISTORTION

(I'm addressing this issue just to have some fun and lighten up my day.)

Then there is that mountain of land use regulation information that someone thought would sound legal but actually makes little or no sense at all:

> "In the event that a written protest against a proposed regulatory specific plan is filed in the office of the Planning and Development Department or with the City Clerk no later than seven days following Planning Commission action by the owners of twenty percent or more, either of the area of the lots included in such proposed plan or of those immediately adjacent in the rear thereof extending one hundred fifty feet therefrom, or of those adjacent to any one side and extending one hundred fifty feet therefrom, or of those directly opposite thereto extending one hundred fifty feet from the street frontage of such opposite lots, such specific plan shall not become effective except by the favorable vote of three-fourths of all the members of the City Council of the City of Phoenix."[51]

READING FORMULA

The Flesch Reading Ease Formula is the standard readability formula used by many federal agencies. It can accurately assess the difficulty of any reading passage written in English. The test results range from zero to one hundred.

- Scores between ninety and one hundred are easy to read by fifth-graders.
- Scores between sixty and seventy are easy to read by eighth- and ninth-graders.
- Scores between zero and thirty are easy to read by college graduates.

The United Kingdom's Government Digital Service says that

government should be an authoritative, trusted source—that means government needs to write in a way everybody understands.

The Service goes on to say, "[w]riting guru Ann Wylie describes research showing that when average sentence length is 14 words, readers understand more than 90% of what they're reading. At 43 words, comprehension drops to less than 10%.[52]

I would say: "A government agency that writes a 134 word sentence in a document meant to serve the public, is out of touch."

"It's no secret that many Americans are lousy writers. Just ask any college professor or employer, including those at prestigious institutions. . . . In 2011, a nationwide test found that only 24 percent of students in eighth and 12th grades were proficient in writing."[53]

BAD WRITING

I looked up "bad writing" on the internet but couldn't find a good example of what I was looking for, so I fell back on my own experience. Many years ago, I wrote a report that addressed a technical issue. When I presented the finished report to the client, I sensed a note of displeasure. So, I asked the client what was bothering him. He answered me as follows: "Well, it's just not what we expected. It cost us a lot of money, you understand. But it's lacking something. What I mean is it's not very technical. Even I can understand it."

It saddened me to think that an adult American had grown up thinking that understandable writing was somehow inferior to gobbledygook, wordy and generally unintelligible jargon.[54]

Since that incident of long ago, I've found that American writing has continued to deteriorate to the point where the federal government has had to adopt the Plain Writing Act of 2010. "The law requires that federal agencies use clear government communication that the public can understand and use."[55]

FUNCTIONAL ILLITERACY

"Approximately 32 million adults in the United States can't read, according to the U.S. Department of Education and the National Institute of Literacy. The Organization for Economic Cooperation and Development found that 50 percent of U.S. adults can't read a book written at an eighth-grade level."[56]

PROFESSIONAL ILLITERACY

The City of Phoenix's zoning regulations start with the following introduction:

Section 600 General Provisions.

A. The zoning districts, regulations, and the uses that are per-mitted in each zoning district as permitted uses are hereby established. Any use that is not specifically permitted or anal-ogous to those specifically permitted is hereby declared to be a prohibited use and unlawful. A permitted use that is not permitted in any district shall not be considered an accessory use in that district.[57]

From that point onward, the city's zoning regulations continue to deteriorate. Yet nearly everyone in the community, including city staff and the city council, pretend they can read and understand every word.

I am a certified reading teacher. I know from years in the class-room what Americans can and cannot read. For sure, they can't read and understand the City of Phoenix's zoning regulations—but they will never admit it.

I hold a reading teacher certificate from the State of California, and one of my dearest friends taught reading for forty years. We often discuss the decline in literacy.

In the original *Star Trek*, episode 52, "Omega Glory," Captain Kirk reads the preamble from the U.S. Constitution to the inhabitants of a parallel universe, who have forgotten how to read English. Kirk admonishes the aliens, saying, "Down the centuries you have slurred the meaning [of the Constitution.]"

American public school students of today, who no longer learn to write cursive, like the inhabitants of the parallel universe, soon won't be able to read our most precious founding documents—the Declaration of Independence and the Constitution. But they'll be able to text "g2g."

Chapter 12

DISCARD JOKERS

Keeping with my playing card theme, I recommend local jurisdictions discard clutter that only serves to detract from the intent of land use regulation.

DISCARD DEFINITION JOKERS

American folklore perpetuates the belief that there is a legal language. Certainly, law, like any profession, has coined words that have special technical meaning. But the idea that there is a legal way to speak and write is nonsense. With few exceptions, words used in legal writing are the same words we all use. Lawyers just like to write in their own endearing pidgin, but it has no legal basis, it's just plain bad English.

Where a list of definitions appear within land use regulations there should instead be a list of such standard reference works as *Merriam-Webster's Collegiate Dictionary, Black's Law Dictionary,* and *A Planners Dictionary.*

DISCARD ZONING ADMINISTRATOR JOKERS

In many jurisdictions, a zoning administrator is given the authority to make planning permit decisions. If a planning permit applicant is dissatisfied with the zoning administrator's decision, the applicant has the right to appeal the decision to the next higher authority. If you eliminate the zoning administrator, you eliminate an unnecessary functionary.

It is a good idea to simplify decision-making by eliminating unnecessary decision-making steps. Paid staff should not be making decisions elected or appointed members of the public have been entrusted to make:

- Legislative planning permits—city council
- Adjudicative planning permits—planning commission
- Ministerial planning permits—decision-making body as required by state law

DISCARD ZONING BOARD OF ADJUSTMENT JOKERS

Generally, the board of adjustment is an appointed body established to:

- hear appeals of decisions made by the zoning administrator;
- interpret unclear land use regulation provisions; and
- decide whether to allow variances from land use regulations.

You don't need a zoning board of adjustments if you adopt clear, concise, and understandable land use regulations. So, stop issuing questionable variances and get rid of the zoning board of adjustment.

DISCARD TEMPORARY USE JOKERS

Nothing devalues zoning regulations as quickly as cluttering up the planning permit process with temporary activities that are neither planning nor zoning related.

Temporary activities are not land use regulations—they don't run with the land:

- **Planning permits run with the land**: They move from deed to deed as the land is transferred from one owner to another.
- **Temporary uses run with the license or permit holder**: They

are "any right or interest that an individual has in movable things."[58] Temporary activities should be generally treated as licenses and be issued by the city clerk or some other functionary at city hall.

DISCARD PERSONAL PROPERTY

Many secondary land uses do not require a building permit (BLD) and a certificate of occupancy (COO) because they are personal property, not real property. Personal property can be any asset other than real estate; personal property is movable. Real estate consists of land, buildings, and natural resources such as crops, minerals, or water; real estate is immovable.

The following are examples of movable personal property:

- Kennel for dogs or cats, hen house for poultry, planter for vegetable gardening
- Swing and slide playhouse, trampoline, and the like
- Vegetable gardens including hothouse, hydroponic, or rooftop
- Office space incidental to managing a primary use
- Incidental services such as a dining room, barber shop, beauty shop, or hobby shop within senior citizen housing, for use by residents
- Customer-pleasing diversions such as theatrical performances, seasonal displays, music, exhibits, and the like to enhance the shopping experience
- Farmers markets selling fresh local foods on private property, including:
  - on-site farming (often, hothouse, hydroponic, or rooftop);
  - on-site aquaculture (indoor or outdoor); or
  - on-site poultry (such as the USDA exempts producers selling less than 20,000 poultry per year).

Regulation of personal property is within the purview of the police powers of the jurisdiction and may require a business license. Let the city clerk worry about barking dogs, crowing roosters, and hemp.

DISCARD TEMPORARY VENDOR PERMIT JOKERS

Every planner I've ever met would be perfectly happy to let the city clerk or some other government functionary deal with street fairs, festivals, exhibitions, flea markets, roach coaches, Christmas tree and pumpkin lots, and high school car washes. All of these are irksome business licenses.

DISCARD HOME OCCUPATION JOKERS

I've never seen a zoning ordinance without a home occupation listing. Home occupation regulation is nonsense. If anyone knows you're working at home, you're in trouble already. If your home occupation complies with homeowner association or deed restriction rules, city hall won't know you're quietly working away in your spare room. On the other hand, the IRS says:

> Whether you are self-employed or an employee, if you use a portion of your home for business, you may be able to take a home office deduction. . . . Generally, in order to claim a business deduction for your home, you must use part of your home exclusively and regularly as your principal place of business or as a place to meet or deal with patients, clients or customers in the normal course of your business.[59]

Where I live, home occupation permits come with loading zone parking permits. The parking permit lets me park in the alley behind my favorite Starbucks, so the fee for the license is well worth the money.

What about cottage industries? "A cottage industry is a small-scale, decentralized manufacturing business often operated out of a home rather than a purpose-built facility."[60] I know a potter who works from home—the kiln requires 440 volts of electricity, and material and finished pots take up the entire backyard. A cottage industry is also another adjudicative planning permit you can add to your list—cottage industry proposal (CIP). It's a form of conditional use permit (CUP).

DISCARD YARD SALES JOKERS

On Friday afternoon, you go out and illegally staple garage sale signs on neighborhood power poles; then, on Saturday morning, you pile up all of your junk on your driveway so people who have nothing better to do can drop by to see what they can buy for little or nothing. Who is going to stop you from doing this? The city planner? The police? The code enforcement officer? None of the above? Get real! City employees have better things to do on weekends, and city hall isn't about to pay them to run around all over town on their off days ticketing taxpaying voters for trying to rid themselves of old worn-out household goods. The last time I responded to a citizen complaint about a garage sale, I ended up at the police chief's house. I bought a folding patio chair.

DISCARD POLITICALLY CORRECT JOKERS

A few years ago, the City of Turlock, California, set out to prevent Walmart from building a superstore in the community. To block Walmart, the city added a definition of a discount superstore to its land use regulations:

A "Discount Superstore" is:

a store that is similar to a "Discount Store" . . . with the exception that [it] also contain[s] a full-service grocery department under the same roof that shares entrances and exits with the discount store area. Such retail stores exceed 100,000 square feet of gross floor area and devote at least five percent (5%) of the total sales floor area to the sale of non-taxable merchandise . . . [61]

Then Turlock amended its land use regulations to exclude discount superstores and to allow membership stores, such as Costco Wholesale, to continue to operate "on the grounds that their customers shop infrequently and buy in bulk, and therefore do not jam traffic." That is a shamefully biased way to administer zoning.[62]

DISCARD TENANT SPECIFIC JOKERS

The attempt to list every variety of desirable business is an exercise in futility. The North American Industry Classification System (NAICS) lists sixty-eight retail store types.[63] Some Euclidian land use regulations seem to find only a handful of businesses to list—certainly not enough to be representative.

A planning permit runs with the land, not with the business. In the following case, the planning permit application was a "request to construct a 7,453-square-foot commercial building for O'Reilly Automotive Stores, Inc. . . . for the retail sale of auto parts, in the Commercial General (CG-1) zone."[64]

So, what were the unique characteristics of the retail auto parts store? The building in question was a 7,453-square-foot box that could have been used to house any sort of commercial activity. In fact, once the planning permit was issued, the applicant acquired the legal right to sell the real property with the permit attached because a planning permit always runs with the land, not with the business. In this case, O'Reilly Automotive Stores had no obligation to occupy the building or to sell retail auto parts. Who knows? By next year, the store could be just another tattoo parlor or payday loan trap.

Smart jurisdictions know that businesses come and go with the wind. So, they don't bend their architectural standards to please individual businesses. One swanky town I'm familiar with requires the same high-quality architecture for every commercial building. So, when a business fails or moves on, the building becomes immediately available for a new tenant, without extensive remodeling—it's hard to disguise those golden arches.

DISCARD PUBLIC ART JOKERS

City hall searched high and low for a public art sculpture that would express the jurisdiction's desire to be the high-tech capital of Silicon Valley. The arts commission, after reviewing dozens of works of contemporary fine art, finally found the perfect *objet d'art*, a weathered steel statue called *Wires of Technology*, expressing the technological breakthroughs anticipated in the decades to come.

Upon purchasing the piece, the arts commission joined with its community partners to bring the spectacular artwork to the city's central park for a Sunday afternoon viewing and learning event. The event was a great success, with attendance in the hundreds. Everyone went home pleased with the results.

On Monday morning, a cleanup crew arrived at the park to remove all of the debris left behind by the hundreds of participants. The park was left in quite a state of disarray; wastepaper, plastic bottles, aluminum cans, uneaten food, and even disposable diapers were everywhere, and a big tangle of bent up, rusted steel was left behind.

On Tuesday morning, the art commission's work crew came back to the park to move the sculpture, *Wires of Technology*, to its permanent home. The sculpture was gone. The crew immediately called the police.

The police investigation eventually got around to questioning city hall's cleanup crew, who complained about the tangle of scrap metal some miscreant dumped in the park sometime over the weekend and how much work it took to cut it up and take it to the dump.

Planners should stay away from public art; they should remove it from land use regulations and shift it to an arts commission or a civic group. Old Dixie is currently facing the predicament of what to do with once-popular Civil War monuments. It's not a good idea for a planning department to get involved in arguments or disputes over public art.

Chapter 13
HOLD ACES

Hold on to your aces; they refine and strengthen land use controls. The more aces, the better.

HOLD ACES THAT REGULATE BUSINESS ACTIVITY

Historically, Euclidian zoning has tried to regulate every aspect of business, but that always fails because there are too many types of distinctly defined businesses—not even the Small Business Administration can keep track of them all.

Municipalities adhering to Euclidian land use regulations, which are unable to deal with all of the many types of businesses, typically end up choosing a few and pretending they are representative of all businesses:

- Group A: Retailing such as hardware, drugs, furniture, apparel, sundries, liquor, bakery, and grocery.
- Group B: Personal services such as beauty salon, barber, day spa, gymnasium, laundry, or dry cleaner.
- Group C: Food services such as restaurant, café, delicatessen, soda fountain, or sandwich shop.
- Group D: Business services such as insurance, real estate, printing, or post office.

- Group E: Education and entertainment such as movie rentals, books and periodicals, hobby and crafts, or collectibles.

Unfortunately, the groups A through E are never complete and never address all types of business activity. What ever became of movie rentals? "At its peak in 2004, Blockbuster had nearly 60,000 employees and over 9,000 stores."[65]

The International Franchise Association alone represents more than 780,000 franchise establishments in over 300 different business format categories.[66] How would your jurisdiction ever be able to address all 300? Trying to control every kind of business activity is an act of futility.

The International Building Code categorizes structures primarily for building and fire code enforcement. The code is concerned with the design and installation of building systems. The code lists structural and fire safety provisions for commercial, industrial, and large residential buildings. The International Building Code covers subjects such as building height and area, foundation, wall, and roof construction, fire protection systems (sprinkler system requirements and design), construction materials, and elevators. The code also addresses Americans with Disabilities Act accommodations.

It seems to me that it would be simpler to just substitute building code groups for business activity groups.

The International Building Code lists seven groups of structures based on physical properties, rather than on products, services, brand names, or ownership.

- Assembly (Group A): Places used for people gathering for entertainment, worship, and eating or drinking.
- Business (Group B): Places where services are provided.
- Educational (Group E): Schools and day care centers up to the twelfth grade.

- Factory (Group F): Places where goods are manufactured or repaired.
- Dangerous (Group H): Places involving production or storage of flammable or toxic materials.
- Institutional (Group I): Places where people are physically unable to leave without assistance.
- Mercantile (Group M): Places where goods are displayed and sold.
- Residential (Group R): Places providing accommodations for overnight stay. (Does not apply to single-family buildings.)
- Storage (Group S): Places where items are stored.

Each building code group specifies materials and safety measures needed to protect end users, rather than trying to figure out some sort of abstract value, such as "sale of new clothing vs. sale of used closing" or "men's hair cutting vs. ladies' hair cutting."

It is not all that difficult to control the size, shape, and structural characteristics of a building. Is seems to me that using the International Building Code Groups or something similar would be a more effective land use control.

HOLD ACES THAT CONTROL ARCHITECTURAL STYLE AND APPEARANCE

Many jurisdictions do what they can to control the looks of buildings through zoning provisions. Some go so far as to insist on a community-wide theme. Themed towns use their themed appearance to attract tourists, express local values, further the arts, preserve history, etc. Theming or branding creates community identity, something every community needs. It may also serve to repurpose a community after the loss of some major economic activity. All over America, there are communities that use theme and branding aces to set themselves apart; many of them have been notably successful.

- Leavenworth, Washington—Bavarian-styled village
- Holland, Michigan—Dutch American heritage
- Solvang, California—Danish-style architecture
- New Glarus, Wisconsin—Swiss pioneer settlement
- Frankenmuth, Michigan—Bavarian-style architecture
- St. Augustine, Florida—Spanish colonial architecture
- Lindsborg, Kansas—Swedish heritage
- Helen, Georgia—Bavarian-style buildings[67]

I've only visited two of these towns—Leavenworth and Solvang—and over decades of smart planning, I've seen both locales transition from rude caricatures to sophisticated memes aimed at replicating culturally correct architectural themes. Now, both locales are importing buildings and motifs from Europe.

Theming has led jurisdictions all over the country to discover that architectural style and appearance are easier to control through planning than through zoning. Theming takes a lot of coordination and agreement.

The planning option gives jurisdictions the choice of using a planned unit development, a general plan, a specific plan, or a form-based code to control the look and feel of the community. Planning makes it much easier to create a community brand or to preserve local heritage.

. . . after the failed uprising of August 1944, Adolf Hitler personally ordered that the entire city be razed to the ground. . . . Eighty-five percent of the greater city was destroyed, while Old Warsaw and the Royal Castle were reduced to their foundations.

Remarkably, the Poles set about rebuilding the centre of Warsaw exactly as it had looked before the war. They went to extraordinary lengths, studying 18th-century views by Canaletto and Marcello Bacciarelli, and even travelling to Blenheim

Palace to copy the great door lock, which was known to be a duplicate of the one at the Royal Castle.[68]

There is nothing to stop any community from rebuilding grandeur after a disaster or even after decades of neglect or misguided attempts at modernization.

Chapter 14

PLANNING PERMISSION

The public is under the misapprehension that there are many different kinds of planning permissions. But over the years, state laws and court cases have suggested that all planning permission falls into one of three categories: legislative, adjudicative, and ministerial.

In case law, these three terms appear repeatedly. On the other hand, the three terms are almost never mentioned in zoning and subdivision regulations. It's as if planners and lawyers work with completely different subject matter, with no common language whatsoever.

The remainder of this chapter is taken directly from my book *Fight City Hall and Win: How to Defend Your Community Against Rapacious Developers, Scared Bureaucrats, and Corrupt Politicians.*

LEGISLATIVE, ADJUDICATIVE, AND MINISTERIAL

Based on the accumulation of court opinions you can be assured that you don't need an open-ended list of processes that go on and on forever, and you don't need to resort to issuing magical land use entitlements.

Explanation by analogy. I'll try to explain the difference between legislative, adjudicative, and ministerial by analogy: buying a car, getting a driver's license, and registering a car, all fun things to do.

Buying your new car—a legislative action. Say you want to trade in your old gas-guzzler for a new hybrid. You go to a car dealer and find a ride you like. Now you have to haggle with the car dealer to make a deal. You have no obligation to buy the car from this particular dealer. On the other hand, the dealer has no obligation to sell you the car. You can refuse to pay the sticker price, and the dealer can refuse to sell you the car for less. Neither of you is under any obligation to make a deal. But if you and the car dealer decide to work together to reach an agreement, everything is negotiable: Options can be added or subtracted from the car. The dealer can refuse to take your car as a trade-in. You can ask for an extended warranty and a free tank of gas. The dealer can refuse to finance the purchase of the car or ask you to pay for undercoating.

Whether or not you reach accord is strictly between you and the car dealer. You don't have to buy a car from that dealer, and that dealer does not have to sell a car to you.

Obtaining a driver's license—an adjudicative action. Obtaining a driver's license is an adjudicative action. To obtain a driver's license, you have to pass a driver's test. But even if you pass the test, you may be restricted as to the type of vehicle or the time of day you may drive or even the kinds of roads you may drive on. The issuing agency may add all sorts of binding conditions, such as requiring you to wear glasses, not allowing you to drive after dark, or keeping you from driving on freeways. Not all drivers' licenses are equal. Some allow you to drive a car, others a motorcycle or a truck. You may even be allowed to upgrade your license so you can drive a commercial vehicle, an emergency vehicle, or a school bus.

Registering your new car—a ministerial action. A ministerial action is like registering that new car you just bought. You take your new car down to the motor vehicle office, where it must be inspected. The registrar verifies that your ownership documents are in order, checks your car's serial number, makes sure your car has seat belts, air bags, and all of its parts. If your car complies with every item on the checklist, it is automatically registered. If it is missing even one item on the checklist, it does not qualify for registration. It's yes or no. The inspector has no authority to issue a registration for a car that fails to pass the checklist.

ANOTHER ATTEMPT TO EXPLAIN

Let's look at that again from another angle.

Another example—a legislative action. You come up with a great idea for a development project. You take your idea to city hall. City hall looks at your idea and says it requires a legislative action: the general plan has to be changed to accommodate your idea. If, for any reason, city hall doesn't like your idea, it can just say no. However, you may negotiate with city hall and make changes to your project to come up with something city hall likes. You can add features, change the size, move things around, or offer city hall a sweetener such as a donation of parkland or a school site. City hall can ask to see your financial records, check your credit rating, and look at other projects you have built or talk to people about your character. You and city hall are free to work out a deal that satisfies both sides.

Another example—an adjudicative action. You always have a right to use your land within the limits spelled out in the land use regulations.

City hall always has a right to review your project to make sure you meet certain objective standards, such as height limit, setback distance from the side and rear property lines, and conformance to zoning. If your project meets all standards and criteria specified in the code or can be modified to meet the standards and criteria, city hall must allow you to proceed with your project.

But if your application doesn't meet all of city hall's objective standards and criteria, city hall may deny your application or add conditions to your application to bring it into conformity with all of its objective standards and criteria. City hall always has the right to ask you to redesign your proposal so it will fit into the neighborhood without harming the value of other properties. To accomplish this, city hall may restrict hours of operation, require you to use a toned-down paint scheme, or keep you from making too much noise. All sorts of modifiers can be added to match your proposal to the site and surrounding neighborhood.

Another example—a ministerial action. You have subdivided your land and now you want to finalize the subdivision. City hall requires you to submit a plat (or final subdivision map) drawn to scale, which includes:

- scale, north arrow, name and phone number of person preparing the plan;
- existing and proposed lot lines and lot areas;
- building pad elevations and adjacent grades within 100 feet of project boundary; and
- location, dimensions, and use of structures.

If your plat or map complies with all of the requirements, city hall grants your planning permit. If anything is missing or incorrect, city hall denies your permit. It's just yes or no.

BLESSED SIMPLIFICATION

Every planning permit issued by the planning department is legislative, adjudicative, or ministerial. There shouldn't be any exceptions to this rule. Legislative, adjudicative, and ministerial; that's all there is to it. Simple, really.

Chapter 15
PLANNING PERMIT APPEAL

Any person aggrieved by a planning permit decision may appeal the decision to the next higher authority. Appeals can be greatly reduced by eliminating the zoning administrator and moving decision-making up one notch: have the planning commission make decisions on adjudicative planning permits, and have the city council make decisions on legislative planning permits.

Shortening the decision-making path is especially advantageous where state law limits the entire appeal period to sixty days.

But always remember, a well written and fully documented staff report is the key to reducing the number of appeals. Applicants tend to appeal a decision when they think they have a good chance of winning. If the planning department writes ironclad staff reports, few applicants will be inclined to challenge them.

Chapter 16

THE VARIANCE

The Tenth Amendment to the United States Constitution says that "[t]he powers not delegated to the United States by the Constitution, nor prohibited by it to the states, are reserved to the states respectively, or to the people."[69]

RESERVED FOR THE STATES

Planning and zoning powers are reserved for the states or the people.[70]

Basis for land-use planning authority. "The police power is the basis for land-use planning authority in the United States."[71] "The authority for use of police power under American Constitutional law has its roots in English and European common law traditions."[72]

State by state land use regulations. Under the constitution, each state adopts its own land use regulations with little participation by the federal government—that is why zoning variance regulations differ from state to state.

Basic nature of land. Real estate agents remind us to look at the "location, location, location." Land is immovable—land stays put. As long as land doesn't travel across state lines, the federal government has no reason to interfere with an individual state's police power to regulate land use. Hence, there are no nationwide zoning variance regulations.

Common meaning of variance. "A variance is a limited waiver of development standards for a use that is otherwise permitted in that zone. The city or county may grant a variance in special cases where: (1) application of the zoning regulations would deprive property of the uses enjoyed by nearby, similarly zoned lands; and (2) restrictions have been imposed to ensure that the variance will not be a grant of special privilege."[73]

In the Superior Court of Delaware, in the case of *WaWa, Inc. v. New Castle County Board of Adjustments*, found that a variance application seeks permission to use property in a way not allowed by the zoning. Relief can be classified as either "area variance" or a "use variance."

Area Variance. An area variance relaxes incidental limitations to an allowed use—it allows deviation from zoning restrictions such as the height, lot coverage, size of buildings, placement of a building on the site or other restrictions relating to physical characteristics of the site. An area variance is subjected to the "exceptional practical difficulty" test.

Use Variance. A use variance allows a property to be used in a way prohibited in the zoning district. A use variance is subjected to the "unnecessary hardship" test.[74]

TEST TO ESTABLISH RELIEF

A variance application seeking permission to use property in a way not allowed by the zoning must pass a test before relief may be granted:

Area variance "exceptional practical difficulty" test. An area variance may be granted when the physical characteristics of the property make strict compliance with the land use regulations impractical, such as "where the rear half of a lot is a steep slope, a variance might be approved to allow a house to be built closer to the street than usually allowed."[75] Or, the problem is caused by something only applicable to the specific property. "The classic justification for a variance is that the unique physical conditions of the land involved such as a steep slope or the presence of wetlands make it impractical to meet the precise setbacks required . . ."[76]

Use variance "unnecessary hardship" test. The legal test requires the owner to show that strict compliance would prevent any reasonable use of the property.[77]

In deciding to grant a [use] variance, the objective finding of fact must determine that:

- The problem is caused by strict application of the land use regulations.[78] Recent decisions now allow consideration of reasonable accommodation for a disabled person.[79]
- The problem is caused by something that is not self-induced or self-created. For example, buying a property for a purpose the buyer knows is not allowed in the zoning district or selling part of a parcel, then seeking a variance to develop the remainder.
- The problem is caused by something peculiar or unique only to the single property. If the hardship "is common to a number of properties, a zoning amendment, not a variance, is the proper remedy."[80]

THOUGHTS ON ISSUING VARIANCES

The need to issue variances is more about failure than success— failure to communicate, failure to apply logic and failure to comply with the rule of law:

- David W. Owens and Adam Bruggemann, in *A Survey of Experience with Zoning Variances*, say: "The courts have established a detailed and strict interpretation of the statutory requirements a petitioner must meet to qualify for a zoning variance and have, to a lesser extent, elaborated on the negative community impacts variances must avoid."[81]

- James F. Scales, writing in *Practical Advice for Variances*, says: "It is sometimes said that 90% of the variances which are granted should have been denied."[82]

- To the above, I would add: "The need to issue so many variances can be traced back to inadequate local plans and poorly written land use regulations. You won't need a zoning administrator or a zoning board of adjustments if you adopt clear, concise, and understandable land use regulations

Chapter 17

PLANNER'S STAFF REPORT

Most cities now use a consolidated planning permit application that allows an applicant to submit a complex proposal as a single action. This is often called a "one stop" application procedure. The consolidated planning permit application is made possible by breaking the application into two parts:

- General information
- Specific information

General information. This part asks the applicant to provide name, address, telephone number, and other general information regarding the proposal.

Specific information. This part asks for detailed information such as layout, design, or parking needs. Many jurisdictions fail to ask the applicant to submit enough of the right kind of detailed information. Without the details, staff can't write an effective staff report. Unfortunately, that is precisely why some jurisdictions don't ask for detailed information—corrupt to the core.

STAFF REPORT ANALYSIS

Legislative decisions and adjudicative decisions are processed using similar-looking staff report formats. The main difference between the two is the need to address a finding of fact based on the record of the proceedings.

Finding of fact—sometimes. A legislative staff report requires a finding of fact only if it is required by state law.

Finding of fact—always. An adjudicative staff report always requires a finding of fact.

Finding of fact—content. The finding of fact must explain the basis on which the decision was made, the facts discovered in the public hearing, and the reasons justifying the decision based on the facts and objective rules, standards, and criteria.

Finding of fact—substantiality. The administrative record must contain substantial evidence in support of the finding of fact. Substantial evidence is evidence that "a reasonable mind could accept as adequate to support a conclusion."[83]

Finding of fact—checklist. The case planner, assisted by other city staff, needs to go through the planning permit application and isolate each point the applicant presents. Then, the planner must address each of the following points.

- ☐ Does the application contain all of the information required, in sufficient detail, to explain the scope of the proposal and disclose its social, economic, and environmental effects on the community?
- ☐ Is there a public need for the proposal?
- ☐ Will the proposal be detrimental to public health, safety, or welfare?
- ☐ Will the proposal produce a social environment of stable and desirable character?
- ☐ Will the proposal produce an economic environment of stable and desirable character?

☐ Is the proposal premature; for example, will it open undeveloped land to development before the city can supply adequate services?

☐ Is the scale and density of the proposal compatible with surrounding development?

☐ Is the scale and density of the proposal compatible with the natural environment?

☐ Is the scale and density of the proposal compatible with the wider community?

☐ Will the proposal lower the livability rating (suitability for human living) of the community, based on available facts? (See Maslow's hierarchy of needs.)

☐ Is there a feasible better alternative than the proposal as submitted?

☐ Have all feasible alternatives been explored and rejected based on the proposal's superior attributes and benefit to end users and the wider community?

☐ Does the proposal violate design standards applicable to the site?

☐ Will the application deprive nearby property owners of the enjoyment of their property?

☐ Is the size and shape of the site adequate to accommodate the proposal?

☐ Is the proposal properly designed for the site in regard to improvements, vehicle access, and internal traffic circulation, pedestrian access, setbacks, height and bulk of buildings, walls and fences, landscaping, screening, exterior lighting, and signs?

☐ Will the proposal subject neighbors to excessive glare from lights?

☐ Will the proposal subject neighbors to excessive noise from mechanical devices?

☐ Will the proposal subject neighbors to excessive noise from human activities?

☐ Will the proposal generate more traffic than local streets can safely carry without congestion?

☐ Is there sufficient public-school capacity available to supply the application, based on available facts and the testimony of providers?

☐ Is there sufficient police protection capacity available to supply the application, based on available facts and the verifiable testimony of providers?

☐ Is there sufficient fire and rescue capacity available to supply the application, based on available facts and the verifiable testimony of providers?

☐ Are there sufficient library, recreational, and other municipal amenities available to supply the proposal, based on available facts and the verifiable testimony of providers?

☐ Is there sufficient electricity available to supply the application, based on available facts and the verifiable testimony of providers?

☐ Is there sufficient natural gas available to supply the proposal, based on available facts and the testimony of providers?

☐ Is there sufficient potable water available to supply the application, based on available facts and the verifiable testimony of providers?

☐ Is there sufficient sanitary sewer capacity available to supply the application, based on available facts and the verifiable testimony of providers?

☐ Is there sufficient storm drainage capacity available to supply the application, based on available facts and the verifiable testimony of providers?

☐ Were all public notices adequate? "[T]he courts view inadequate notice as equivalent to providing no notice at all."[84]

☐ Were all responsible agencies (utility providers, cemetery district, etc.) notified?

☐ Were all facts and legal points available at the time contained in the staff report presented to the hearing body?

APPELLATE COURT RULINGS

☐ The California Court of Appeal, in *Novi v. City of Pacifica*, ruled that city hall may reject an application if it is detrimental to the community's well-being.[85]

☐ Is the proposal detrimental to the health, safety, morals, comfort, and general welfare of persons residing or working in your neighborhood?[86]

☐ Will the proposal be injurious or detrimental to property and improvements in the neighborhood?

☐ Will the proposal damage the general welfare of the city?

☐ Will the proposal impair the value of land and buildings in the neighborhood?

☐ Will the proposal lack variety in its design of structures and grounds?

☐ Will the proposal be monotonous in its external appearance? (See *Slate*, "The Generic City";[87] and *The Cut*, "The Psychological Cost of Boring Buildings."[88])

THE VARIANCE

The following questions are applicable to a variance only:

☐ Will strict application of land use regulations deprive the property of privileges enjoyed by other properties in the vicinity that have the identical zoning classification?

☐ Are there special circumstances, such as size, shape, topography, location, or surroundings, that deprive the property of privileges enjoyed by other properties in the identical zoning classification?

☐ Will the preservation and enjoyment of a substantial property right be lost if the variance is denied?

☐ Will extraordinary hardship result from strict compliance with the land use regulations if the variance is denied?

☐ Will denial of the variance be detrimental to the public health, safety, or welfare or be injurious to other properties in the vicinity?

☐ Will granting the variance circumvent any provisions of the land use regulations?

☐ Will the variance grant more than a minimum deviation from the land use regulations?

☐ Is there no practical alternative to granting the variance?

OBJECTIVE STANDARDS FOR DECISION-MAKING

Each jurisdiction must have written objective standards for adjudicative approval or denial of each category of discretionary planning permit. The planning department is supposed to be the caretaker of these city council–approved objective standards for decision-making.

CONDITIONS AND LIMITATIONS

In granting a discretionary planning permit, the hearing body may impose reasonable conditions or limitations it deems necessary to ensure compliance with general plan criteria or objective rules and objective standards of land use regulation.

The following are examples of conditions the hearing body may impose:

☐ Limit the way the use is conducted, such as limiting outdoor seating.

☐ Regulate noise, vibration, and odor.

☐ Regulate hours during which certain activities may occur.

☐ Establish a schedule for completing construction.

☐ Increase lot size, yard dimensions, or open space or require environmental buffering.

☐ Require installation of fences, walls, or landscape screening.

☐ Regulate glare from outdoor lighting.

☐ Require landscaping and landscape maintenance to preserve the aesthetics of the surrounding area.

☐ Modify street width or designate the location and number of vehicle access points.

☐ Require pedestrian, disabled, and bicycle pathways to serve the property.

☐ Modify off-street parking and loading requirements.

☐ Specify parking lot and sidewalk surface materials.

☐ Limit size, location, and number of signs.

☐ Limit location, coverage, or height of structures.

☐ Limit or prohibit openings in structures.

☐ Require enclosure of storage and limit outside display.

Yes, there are communities that ask these questions, and more. They are our nation's most desirable places to live.

Chapter 18
MAIL MERGE FORMS

Mail merge creates personalized word processing documents that combine fixed text templates with variable data sources.

Mail merge works using only a few simple steps:

- Create a fixed text document.
- Create a data source with merge fields.
- Insert the merge field data into the fixed text document.
- Output a seamless personalized document.

If you don't want to economize and use the free mail merge software that came with your computer, you can squander tens of thousands of dollars on custom software from a vendor. It's up to you—free or fee.

THE ADMINISTRATIVE RECORD

City hall is required to maintain a complete record of every written, visual, and oral document associated with a planning permit application.

Curtin's California Land Use and Planning Law (a book that provides a summary of California's land use and planning laws but generally gives advice that applies nationwide) states the following about administrative records for planning permit applications:

For land use decisions, the [administrative] record normally will include application materials, memos and correspondence to and from staff, notices, agendas, staff reports, minutes, transcripts of proceedings, all documents presented to the decision-making body by staff, applicant, or others, and proposed and final versions of findings, resolutions, and ordinances.[89]

Nearly all of the administrative record is made up of paperwork generated in the planning department, either by hand or by computer. If you write everything by hand, over and over again for every planning permit application, the paperwork will become drudgery of the third kind.

If you use mail merge to assemble the administrative record from my twenty-three fixed text document forms and thirty-six data sources, the planning permit application paperwork can be completed in less than one hour, including a coffee break—it's merely a question of how much time you want to waste doing drudge work.

Fixed Text Forms	
1. Application Form	13. CC Notice Response Letters
2. 30-Day Letter	14. CC Staff Report
3. PC Notification	15. CC Packet Mailing
4. PC Declaration of Posting	16. CC Final Ordinance
5. PC Public Notice	17. CC Final Resolution
6. Response Letters	18. CC Action Letter
7. PC Staff Report	19. Miscellaneous
8. PC Packet Mailing	20. Annex Response Agency
9. PC Final Resolution	21. Environmental Assessment
10. PC Action Letter	22. Notice of Exemption
11. CC Public Notice	23. Improvement Plan Checklist
12. Declaration of Posting	

Variable Data Sources
Data file: 01_permit_type.rtf
Data file: 02_permit type_CAPS.rtf
Data file: 03_case_identification_number.rtf
Data file: 04_planning_permit_identification.rtf
Data file: 05_owner_name_and_address.rtf
Data file: 06_agent_name_and_address.rtf
Data file: 07_project_location_address.rtf
Data file:08_proposal_location_and_address_CAPS.rtf
Data file: 09_application_identification_block.rtf
Data file: 10_NEPA_status.rtf
Data file: 11_application_completion_date.rtf
Data file: 12_date_30_day_letter_mailed.rtf
Data file: 13_PC_hearing_date.rtf
Data file: 14_PC_newpaper_posting_date.rtf
Data file: 15_PC_newspaper_publication_date.rtf
Data file: 16_responsible_agency_mailing_date.rtf
Data file: 17_responsible_agency_return_date.rtf
Data file: 18_locality_and_setting.rtf
Data file: 19_proposal_description.rtf
Data file: 20_proposal_analysis.rtf
Data file: 21_surrounding_land_use.rtf
Data file: 22_finding_of_fact.rtf
Data file: 23_advisory_committee_recommendation.rtf
Data file: 24_conditions_building_inspection.rtf
Data file: 25_conditions_code_enforcement.rtf
Data file: 26_conditions_economic_development.rtf
Data file: 27_conditions_fire.rtf
Data file: 28_conditions_parks_recreation.rtf
Data file: 29_conditions_planning.rtf
Data file: 30_conditions_police.rtf
Data file: 31_conditions_public_works.rtf
Data file: 32_PC_resolution_number.rtf
Data file: 33_PC_action_letter.rtf
Data file: 34_CC_hearing_date.rtf
Data file: 35_CC_decision_results.rtf
Data file: 36_CC_action_letter.rtf

Staff report mail merge forms. Not all twenty-nine *fixed text* forms or thirty-six *data files* are used every time you process a planning permit application. Sometimes you can construct your entire staff report using as few as eight *data files*.

Staff reports. So, if you free yourself from drudge work, what will be left for you to do? How about writing accurate and informative staff reports?

The staff report is the heart of planning permit processing. Well-crafted staff reports are often the difference between jurisdictions that attract award-winning real estate developers and jurisdictions that approve anything that comes down the pike.

The staff report template I suggest you use asks for a lot more information than the run-of-the-mill staff report templates most jurisdictions use.

You can download staff report templates from my website, http://commonsensezoning.com.

Both Microsoft Word and Corel Word Perfect come with mail merge features, either one of which is easy to use.

MAIL MERGE STAFF REPORT EXAMPLE

City of Heavenly Bliss Staff Report

Planning Permit: *Insert your data file: permit_type.rtf*

Planning Commission Meeting

Insert your data file: PC_hearing_date.rtf

1. PROJECT IDENTIFICATION

Insert your data file: application_identification_block.rtf

2. PROJECT LOCALITY AND SETTING

Insert your data file: locality_and_setting.rtf

3. PROJECT DESCRIPTION

Insert your data file: proposal_description.rtf

4. TYPE OF ACTION—ADJUDICATIVE

The action has been deemed by the courts to be an adjudicative or quasi-judicial act because it involves the application of a previously legislated rule to a specific set of existing facts.

5. FINDING OF FACT—REQUIRED

A finding of fact is required for an adjudicatory land use matter. The planning commission's written finding of fact must include substantial evidence that *a reasonable mind might accept as adequate* to support the conclusion.

6. PROJECT ANALYSIS

Insert your data file: proposal_analysis.rtf

7. FINDING OF FACT BASED ON SUBSTANTIAL EVIDENCE

Insert your data file: finding_of_fact.rtf

8. RESPONSIBLE AGENCY REGULATORY JURISDICTION

A number of public and private entities, including city and county departments, special districts, and public utilities, have regulatory jurisdiction over a variety of services, utilities, health and educational facilities, and other amenities. These entities are collectively called "responsible agencies."

The planning commission is legally required to include these responsible agencies in the decision-making process. The planning commission is legally obligated to consider recommendations submitted by responsible agencies. Failure to protect the regulatory jurisdiction of responsible agencies can lead to serious problems such as denial of service, inadequate coverage, or lengthened emergency response time. Responsible agency recommendations are presented as "conditions of approval."

9. CITY DEPARTMENTS' CONDITIONS OF APPROVAL

9.1   Building Inspection Conditions, Mr. Magoo: 800.555.9999
      Insert data file: conditions_building_inspection.rtf

9.2   Code Enforcement Conditions, Chief Inspector Clouseau: 800.555.9999
      Insert data file: conditions_code_enforcement.rtf

9.3   Economic Development Conditions, Lehman Brothers: 800.555.9999
      Insert data file: conditions_economic_development.rtf

9.4   Fire Marshall Conditions, Captain John Orr: 800.555.9999
      Insert data file: conditions_fire.rtf

9.5   Parks and Recreation Conditions, Leslie Knope: 800.555.9999
      Insert data file: conditions_parks_recreation.rtf

9.6   Planning Department Conditions, Ernest Egger: 800.555.9999
      Insert data file: conditions_planning.rtf

9.7   Police Department Conditions, Randy Adams: 800.555.9999

Insert data file: conditions_police.rtf

9.8   Public Works Department Conditions, Dan Wooten: 800.555.9999

Insert data file: conditions_public_works.rtf

10. RESPONSIBLE AGENCY CONDITIONS OF APPROVAL

The planning commission's written finding of fact must include assurance that responsible agency regulatory jurisdiction will be safe-guarded—*Insert the complete documentation received from the agency:*

10.1   Air Pollution Control District Conditions, Ms. Breathless: 800.555.9999

10.2   Cemetery District Conditions, Mr. Coffin: 800.555.9999

10.3   Council of Governments Conditions, Mayor Mumbles: 800.555.9999

10.4   County Planning Division Conditions, Ms. Adrift: 800.555.9999

10.5   County Environmental Health Department Conditions, Dr. Dolittle: 800.555.9999

10.6   County Public Works Department Conditions, Mr. Pothole: 800.555.9999

10.7   Electric Company Conditions, Dr. Volta: 800.555.9999.

10.8   Fire District Conditions, Mr. Arson: 800.555.9999

10.9   Gas Company Conditions, Mr. Wind: 800.555.9999

10.10   Irrigation District Conditions, Ms. Waterbank: 800.555.9999

10.11   Local Agency Formation Commission Conditions, Ms. Genesis: 800.555.9999

10.12   Natural Resources Conservation Conditions, Dr. Treehug-ger: 800.555.9999

10.13   Pathogen (rodent/insect) Control Agency Conditions, Dr. McFly: 800.555.9999

10.14   Regional Water Quality Control Board Conditions, Dr. Greywater: 800.555.9999

10.15   School District Conditions, Dean of Students, Ed Rooney: 800.555.9999.

10.16   Solid Waste Company Conditions, Mr. Scraps: 800.555.9999

10.17   State Highway Commission Conditions, Ms. Leadfoot: 800.555.9999

11. COMMENTS RECEIVED FROM THE PUBLIC

The staff report writer needs to process exhibits by making them legible—straighten, crop, resize, rotate, or dehaze them. Then, convert the exhibits to PDF and insert them into the staff report. Readable comments can make a difference in the outcome of the public hearing.

11.1   Comment one.

11.2   Comment two . . . .

12. RECOMMENDATION OPTIONS

The planning commission has the authority to take one of three actions on the application:

12.1   **Recommend approval.** If the application, as submitted, meets all state, county, city, and responsible agency regulations, the planning commission may recommend the city council approve it unconditionally.

12.2   **Recommend conditional approval.** If the application can be reasonably amended to meet all state, county, city, and responsible agency regulations, the planning commission may recommend the city council approve it stipulating certain conditions of approval.

12.3   **Recommend denial.** If the application fails to comply with any state, county, city, and responsible agency regulation or fails to serve the public interest, the planning commission may recommend the city council deny approval.

Insert your data file: advisory_committee_recommendation.rtf

EXHIBIT A: VICINITY MAP

EXHIBIT B: SITE PLAN

EXHIBIT C: DRAFT RESOLUTION

Chapter 19

SIMPLE SOLUTIONS FOR SMALLER CITIES

I was never a gifted student; during my first two years of college, I barely scraped by. Then, I stumbled upon a magic formula that upped my class standing, without getting any smarter: I started sitting in the front row, and when I didn't understand something, I'd raise my hand saying "I don't understand" it led to a modicum of notoriety."

Other students would come up to me after class and say, "I'm glad you asked that question, because I didn't understand it, either."

ASK FOR DIRECTIONS

My grades went up a bit, but what I really learned was that it is culturally unacceptable to admit you don't understand. It's a vanity thing; any wife will tell you that vanity has led to legions of grown men driving around lost, refusing to stop and ask directions.

Vanity has also led to legions of planning commissioners pretending to understand zoning mumbo jumbo no one could possibly understand, then voting to approve ruinous planning permit applications just to save face.

PRETENDING TO KNOW

Common sense land use regulations are the product of my experience watching common folks who lack expertise in zoning flounder around at public hearings, pretending to know what is going on around them when they don't!

ZONING YOU CAN UNDERSTAND

Ordinary folks need land use regulations they can easily understand:

- regulations that make sense to people who lack expertise in zoning;
- regulations that clearly explain the decision-making process;
- regulations that invite ordinary people to participate in governance; and
- regulations that protect communities from scoundrels.

BRIBERY AND CORRUPTION

Planning is rife with bribery and corruption. But then, so is the rest of American government. Consider this media report: "The Corruption Perceptions Index 2018 finds the U.S. in 22nd place . . . Denmark and New Zealand held the top-ranked spots on the list; Syria and Somalia were on the bottom."[90]

The Adam Smith Institute, a prominent domestic policy economic think tank, reminds us that "simple systems which anyone can understand" reduce bribery and corruption in planning.[91] If nothing else, common sense zoning makes it easier for community activists to track planning permit applications, looking for irregularities.

Most of the websites I was able to access were concerned with countering European and Australasian bribery and corruption—emphasis on crime prevention.

On the other hand, American websites seem to be more inclined to report after-the-fact exposés recounting how the police uncovered the crimes—emphasis on sensationalism.

WHY MANY PEOPLE SERVE

Planner's Web, an organization that provides useful, jargon-free information to planners, tells us there are three main reasons why ordinary folks choose to serve as planning commissioners:

- **To have a voice in decision-making**. They have something fairly specific they want to accomplish or a general desire to get involved.
- **To serve the community**. They want to contribute their cognitive surplus time to promoting the common good.
- **To contribute their expertise**. They have a useful skill or knowledge, such as architecture, real estate, or planning.[92]

WHY SOME OTHER PEOPLE SERVE

I've found that there are other top reasons why some folks choose to serve as planning commissioners:

- **To have a voice in decision-making**. They have hidden agendas; they make decisions based on their own philosophical or religious reasoning, rather than on the legal merits of the planning permit application under consideration.
- **To serve themselves**. They use their cognitive surplus time to promote perquisites for themselves—padding expenses accounts, taking useless junkets, misusing public credit cards, or trading on their public position to build business clients.
- **To apply their expertise**. They have a useful skill or knowledge, such as architecture, real estate, or planning, which they use to promote their private business ventures—selling professional services to applicants, rigging bids, or taking kickbacks.

COMMON SENSE FOR YOU AND ME

The next four chapters present common sense zoning in its entirety. I hope you find value in the utilitarian simplicity.

Chapter 20
LAND USE REGULATIONS–
PROCEDURES

Note: I wrote the text in this model based on what I thought would work where I live. I was thinking entirely about me and my community, not you or your community. You will have to write your own text—text that fully addresses your community's issues.

A

Administrative record availability–♠. The administrative record documents the proceedings. It includes the application, public notices, memos, and correspondence to and from staff, meeting agendas, staff reports, minutes of meetings, transcripts of proceedings, drawings, samples of materials, maps, models, slideshows, and proposed and final versions of findings, resolutions, and ordinances.

The administrative record does not contain proprietary information—the entire record is public information, available unedited to the public during regular business hours. It is also available for copying at a price competitive with self-service print shops. And it is available on the internet.

Applicability–♠. These local land use regulations govern land division, land development, and the conduct of business. These local land use regulations also segregate land into zoning districts that encourage the appropriate use of land, stabilize and enhance real property values, prevent fire, provide adequate light and air space, prevent residential overcrowding, prevent traffic congestion, facilitate utility placement, and promote public health, safety, and welfare.

Authority—applicable to public property–♠. To the extent allowed by law, these local land use regulations apply to government-owned property.

Authority—clarification of intent–♠. The planning commission has the authority to interpret the meaning of these local land use regulations regarding appropriate zoning classification of an unlisted land use; determination of requirements for height, building setback, yard dimensions, and land area; unforeseen technological change such as invention, new materials, alternative processes; and the like.

Authority—enacted to regulate–♠. These local land use regulations are enacted under the authority of the state's planning and zoning law.

Authority—general applicability–♠. No structure is to be erected, altered, enlarged, or moved in violation of any provision of these local land use regulations. No land, access way, structure, or premises is to be used in any way not allowed in its zoning district.

Authority—governing regulations–♠. If there is conflict between the provisions of these local land use regulations and other city, county, state, or federal regulations, the more restrictive regulations apply.

Authority—greater restriction intended–♠. If these local regulations impose a greater restriction on land use than required by the state's planning and zoning law or other rules, regulations, easements, covenants, or agreements, these local land use regulations govern.

Authority—land use regulation enforcement–♠. The city council has the duty to enforce these land use regulations and the authority to delegate enforcement to agents such as the planning commission, staff, and outside contractors.

Authority—state regulations govern–♠. These local land use regulations supplement, but do not replace, the state's planning and zoning law. If there is a conflict between these local land use regulations and the state's planning and zoning law, the state regulations govern.

B

C

Code enforcement–♠. Enforcement of the code of ordinances is under the purview of the city attorney. Code enforcement is located in Title _____ of this code of ordinances.

D

Defined concepts—counting time–♠. A day is deemed to be the time that elapses between two successive midnights. In counting days, day one starts at the first midnight following an event such as an application submittal, a posting, or a public hearing. For example: if an application is submitted during the day of the twenty-fourth, the time period starts at the first following midnight. Therefore, the twenty-fifth would be counted as day one (1).

Defined concepts—legal language–♠. The verbose jargon commonly used by lawyers has no legal basis; it is just plain bad English. These local land use regulations are written in Standard English. Words, unless specifically defined, have common dictionary meaning.

Defined concepts—rules of grammar–♠. The masculine includes the feminine and the neuter, and the singular includes the plural. The text is generally written in the singular. If a word or phrase has a specialized or technical meaning, a definition is provided. All other words or phrases are to be interpreted as they are commonly defined in everyday usage. A word defined in the state's planning and zoning law has the same meaning when used in these local land use regulations, unless it is clear that a different meaning is intended.

Defined concepts—source dictionaries–♠. Words used in these local land use regulations, unless specifically defined, come from the following standard reference works:

- *Merriam-Webster's Collegiate Dictionary*
- *Black's Law Dictionary*
- *A Planners Dictionary*
- The state's planning and zoning law

E

F

Fees–♠. The setting of fees and the collection of fees fall under the purview of the city council. Fees collected for processing a planning permit are based on the amount of time city officials, staff, and consultants spend reviewing applications, attending meetings, and supervising work. Fees are based on average situations and not on the exact amount of time and materials used on a specific application. Fees charged for processing a planning permit must be paid at the time the application is submitted. Fees are located in Title _____ of this code of ordinances.

Forms—♠. Application forms and permit processing forms are provided to the applicant by the city. Planning forms are based on state law and local regulations. Planning forms are maintained by staff as authorized by the city council and are periodically revised by staff to reflect changes in law or to keep up with changing permit processing technology. All information requested by the city serves the best interests of the public.

G

H

I

J

K

L

Land uses—contract zoning prohibited—♠. Contract zoning occurs when a property owner agrees to give something of value to the government in exchange for less restrictive zoning. Contract zoning results in one property owner profiting from higher intensity development or higher value development while the government profits from something of value without paying for it. Contract zoning gives a profitable advantage to one property owner while denying the same profitable advantage to property owners who remain in the more restrictive zoning district.

Land uses—nuisance prohibited–♠. Any land use activity that causes an unreasonable amount of noise, dust, smoke, vibration, or electrical interference detectable offsite is prohibited.

Land uses—similar uses allowed–♠. The planning commission may rule that a use not specifically listed as an allowed use in a zoning district be included as an allowed use if the use is of the same general type and similar to allowed uses.

Land uses—spot zoning prohibited–♠. Spot zoning, the zoning of a small area differently from surrounding land, is prohibited.

Land uses—unlawful land uses prohibited–♠. Any structure erected, altered, enlarged, converted, moved, or maintained contrary to the provisions of these local land use regulations is unlawful and deemed to be a public nuisance. Legal action may be taken as provided by law to stop the unlawful action.

M

N

Nonconforming land use–♠. A land use can be disruptive to the well-being of the community if it does not conform to general plan criteria or to the requirements of the zoning district in which it is located. There is a legal obligation to uphold the intent of the local general plan by discouraging nonconformance:

- **Nonconforming use—abandonment ends use–♠.** If a non-conforming use ceases for ninety (90) days, the use is deemed abandoned and must not be resumed.
- **Nonconforming use—construction requirements–♠.** If a nonconforming structure is at least fifty (50) percent destroyed, reconstruction must comply with the regulations for the

zoning district in which it is located. The extent of damage is to be based on the true cash value based on evidence from the county assessor's records for the year preceding destruction.

- **Nonconforming use—deemed nonconforming–♠.** A use lawfully occupying a structure or site is deemed to be non-conforming if it does not conform to the regulations for the zoning district in which it is located.

- **Nonconforming use—maintenance and repairs–♠.** Routine maintenance and repairs may be performed on a nonconforming structure or site.

- **Nonconforming structure—modification prohibited–♠.** A nonconforming structure is not to be moved, altered, or enlarged, unless the action is required by law or the action will eliminate the nonconformance.

- **Nonconforming use—modification prohibited–♠.** No structure is to be moved, altered, or enlarged to facilitate expansion of a nonconforming use.

- **Nonconforming use—right to restrict use–♠.** A nonconforming lot that was legally created may be used as if it were a conforming lot. The extent of land use may, however, be restricted to protect public health, safety, and the general welfare or to implement local plans.

O

P

Planning permit—authorization expiration–♠. Local plans are not static; they change over time and quickly become obsolete. If a planning permit is not used within a short period of time, community needs may change or another project may be prevented from filling the need. It is essential to the community's well-being that projects be quickly completed.

Planning permit—authorization expiration—♠. If the time limit expires and no extension has been granted, the planning permit is voided.

Planning permit—frivolous or nuisance applications—♠. To prevent frivolous or nuisance applications, the applicant must submit the proposed action to staff at a pre-application conference. If staff rules that the proposal is an incomplete idea not fully thought out, an application may not be submitted until staff rules the proposal meets all application requirements and complies with the provisions of all local plans.

Planning permit—held in abeyance—♠. An appeal automatically stays a planning permit until the appeal is completed at the local and court level.

Planning permit—new application limitation—♠. If an application is denied by a decision-making body or an appellate body, it may not be resubmitted for one (1) year from the final disposition, including any appeal, unless the decision to deny specifically states, in writing, that the denial is "without prejudice."

Planning permit—revocation or modification—♠. A planning permit is legal and binding between the applicant and the local jurisdiction. Violating a planning permit is no different from violating any other agreement. If a violation occurs, legal action may be taken to enforce the agreement. At other times, a planning permit may need to be modified to protect the interests of the parties involved.

Planning permit modification Hearing—♠. A planning permit may be modified by the body that authorized it. Doing so requires the body to post notice and hold a hearing in the same manner as required for issuing the planning permit.

Planning permit must comply with conditions–♠. When a planning permit is approved, the applicant must sign the permit acknowledging that they have read, understand, and agree to comply with the conditions of approval. Failure to comply with the conditions of approval is unlawful and punishable.

Planning permit—revocation by issuing body–♠. A planning permit may be revoked by the body that issued it, in the same manner as required for issuing the planning permit. Any one of the following causes is grounds for revocation:

- **Planning permit causes harm or damage.** The planning permit is put into action to the detriment of public safety or constitutes a nuisance.
- **Planning permit endangers public welfare.** The continued operation or effect of the land use endangers public welfare.
- **Planning permit exercised contrary to law.** The planning permit is put into action contrary to the conditions of approval or of any regulation, statute, ordinance, or law.
- **Planning permit obtained by fraud.** The planning permit was obtained by fraud.

Planning permit—time limit–♠. A planning permit becomes void one (1) year after it is granted, unless, within that year, the activity is started and diligently pursued, or unless the state's planning and zoning law specifies a different time limit.

Planning permit—time limit extension–♠. A planning permit time extension may be granted for a maximum of one (1) additional year unless the state's planning and zoning law specifies a different time limit.

Q

R

S

Sign structure nonconformance–♠. A sign structure that was legally erected but does not meet current land use regulation standards is deemed nonconforming:

- **Sign structure—nonconformance restricted–♠.** A nonconforming sign structure is not to be changed, expanded or altered in any way that would increase the degree of nonconformance. A nonconforming sign structure is not to be physically altered to prolong its useful life. Nor is any part of it to be moved to any other location where it would continue to be nonconforming.
- **Sign structure—terminated by amortization–♠.** A nonconforming sign structure not terminated by any other provision of these local land use regulations must be removed by January 1, XXXX.
- **Sign structure—terminated by casualty–♠.** A nonconforming sign structure must be removed if damaged or destroyed to the extent of twenty-five (25) percent of its replacement cost.
- **Sign structure—terminated by change of business–♠.** A nonconforming sign structure that identifies a business must be removed upon change of ownership or control of the business.

T

Those vested with authority—compliance with provisions of law–♠. Elected officials, appointed boards and commissions, staff, and outside contractors vested with the authority to issue planning permits must comply with the provisions of law.

Those vested with authority—planning permit issued in conflict with law–♠. A planning permit issued in conflict with this code of ordinances, intentionally or otherwise, is void.

Those vested with authority—unlawful execution of official act–♠. It is unlawful for a person who is an employee, agent, or a principal in a land use action to officially execute a certificate or affidavit or perform an official act in regard to the same land use action.

Those vested with authority—unlawful performance of official act–♠. It is unlawful for any person to cause or allow construction, alteration, improvement, or use in any manner not in compliance with this code of ordinances or conditions of approval.

U

V

W

X

Y

Z

Zoning districts–♠. These land use regulations provide for eight zones. Most jurisdictions list many more. The intent is to minimize zoning in favor of maximizing planning. Planning sets goals designed to contribute to long-term community success; zoning does little more than designate which land uses are allowed or prohibited.

Zoning Districts	
AR – Acreage Residential	GC – General Commercial
LR – Low-Density Residential	NC – Neighborhood Commercial
MR – Medium-Density Residential	LI – Light Industrial
HR – High-Density Residential	HI – Heavy Industrial

Zoning overlay districts–♠. A zoning overlay district is a designation that may be superimposed on a lot to modify or restrict use without completely removing or negating the lot's zoning district designation.

Zoning Overlay Districts	
GWOD – Greenway Overlay	PDOD – Planned Development Overlay
REOD – Redevelopment Overlay	FPOD – Flood Plain Overlay

Zoning boundary interpretation–♠. The following rules apply when making a boundary determination:

- If a zoning district boundary approximately follows the centerline of a street, alley, or other right-of-way, the centerline is the zoning district boundary.
- If a zoning district boundary approximately follows the centerline of a waterway, the centerline is the zoning district boundary. If the waterway centerline moves as a result of natural erosion and deposition, the zoning district boundary moves with the centerline.
- If a zoning district boundary approximately follows a lot line, the lot line is the boundary.
- If a zoning district boundary divides a lot, the entire lot is deemed to be in the zoning district that allows the least intensive or lowest density of land use.
- If a street, alley, or other public right-of-way is vacated, the zoning districts abutting each side of it are extended to the centerline of the former right-of-way.

- If none of the above rules clarify the zoning district boundary location, the planning commission has the authority to make a boundary determination based on the available evidence.

Zoning map—annual update-♠. The zoning map is revised once a year, effective on January first. A permanent acetate copy of the old zoning map is to be preserved whenever the zoning map is revised.

Zoning map—zoning districts established-♠. The location and boundaries of the zoning districts are hereby established as shown on the map entitled: "City of _____ Zoning Map."

Zoning map—individual planning permit update-♠. An individual planning permit that changes the zoning map goes into effect when passed, but the zoning map will not show the change until the annual revision.

Zoning map—part of land use regulations-♠. The zoning map is deemed to be part of these local land use regulations.

Zoning text—annual update-♠. Zoning text is revised once a year, effective on January first, unless the city council declares the revision to be necessary to protect the general welfare or the common good. An example would be the finding of a previously unknown earthquake fault, a change in federal of state law, or the discovery of a serious flaw in the existing zoning text.

Chapter 21
LAND USE REGULATIONS–PERMITS

There are only three categories of planning permits: legislative, adjudicative, and ministerial. The named subcategories are used by planners because they find it more efficient to process planning permit applications digitally, using standardized media prepared ahead of time and stored for future use. The subcategories are time-saving shortcuts that facilitate cybernation of the workplace.

PLANNING PERMISSION INCLUDING TIME-SAVING SHORTCUTS NAMES

LEGISLATIVE PLANNING PERMITS–♥

(ANX) Annexation (Change of Organization)

    (ANP) Annexation–Preliminary

    (ANL) LAFCO (Local Agency Formation Commission) Processing Annexation

    (ANF) Annexation–Final

(DEV) Development Agreement

(FBC) Form-based Code

(GPA) General Plan Adoption or Amendment

(GPM) General Plan Map Adoption or Amendment

(GPT) General Plan Text Adoption or Amendment

(LCP) Local Coastal Program Adoption or Amendment

(PDZ) Planned Development Zoning

(PRZ) Prezone of Unincorporated Territory

(SPA) Specific Plan Adoption or Amendment

(ZOA) Zoning Ordinance Adoption or Amendment

(ZMA) Zoning Map Adoption or Amendment

(ZTA) Zoning Text Adoption or Amendment

ADJUDICATIVE PLANNING PERMITS–♥

(CDP) Coastal Development Proposal

(CND) Condominium Conversion

(CUP) Conditional Use Permit

(EIS) Environmental Impact Statement

(PDP) Planned Development Proposal

(LLA) Lot Line Adjustment

(PNP) Partition Proposal

(RTA) Reversion to Acreage

(SDR) Site Design Review

(SPX) Subdivision Proposal Exception

(SUB) Subdivision Proposal

(VAR) Variance

MINISTERIAL PLANNING PERMITS–♥

(BLD) Building Permit

(COC) Certificate of Compliance

(COO) Certificate of Occupancy

(ENV) Environmental Assessment

(PTP) Partition Plat

(SDP) Subdivision Plat

(MOP) Merger of Parcels

(PTE) Permit Time Extension

(TME) Subdivision Time Extension

(VRE) Vesting Rights Time Extension

STANDARD PLANNING PERMISSION PROCESSING PROCEDURE–♥

The standard planning permission processing procedure is simple and linear—no participant should have difficulty understanding the procedure:

- **Legislative action**. A legislative action is the exercise of the power to make rules by a body empowered to do so. The legislative body has wide-ranging authority to make or modify rules.
- **Adjudicative action**. An adjudicative or quasi-judicial action is an action that is subject to judgment by the planning commission. The objective is to reach a reasonable settlement of the application for a planning permit. The planning commission must establish the facts and define and interpret the applicable laws.
- **Ministerial action**. A ministerial action is performed in accordance with law and established procedures without exercising any individual judgment or discretion. In judging a planning permit, the law does not allow for judgment or variation.

DECISION-MAKING PROCESS—LEGISLATIVE ACTIONS–♥

Action 1: Pre-application conference. The applicant discusses the proposed project with a committee of planning staff members and others. The committee may meet several times.

Action 2: Application submittal. The applicant submits the proposed project for the planner to review.

Action 3: Statutory review period. The planner reviews the proposed project for XX days. During the review, the planner also determines the proposed project's environmental effects and asks that one of the following documents be submitted for review:

- Categorical Exclusion (CATEX)
- Environmental Finding of No Significant Impact (FONSI)
- Environmental Impact Statement (EIS)

Action 4: Planning commission staff report. The planner reviews the proposed project, then writes a staff report that explains the facts in the matter.

Action 5: Planning commission public notice posting. The planner sends the proposed project and the environmental documentation out for public review. The public has XX days to review and comment.

Action 6: Planning commission public hearing packet. The planner sends a packet containing the proposed project, the environmental documentation, any comments received, and the staff report to the planning commission.

Action 7: Planning commission public hearing as an advisory body. The planning commission acts as an advisory body to the city council by recommending which course of action the city council should take.

Action 8: City council staff report. The planner again reviews the proposed project, the environmental documentation, and any additional comment received, and then revises the staff report as needed to include any new evidence.

Action 9: City council public notice posting. The planner sends out for public review the amended proposed project, the environmental documentation, and a revised staff report. The public usually has XX days to review and comment.

Action 10: City council hearing packet. The planner sends the city council a packet containing the amended proposed project, the environmental documentation, any additional comments received, and the revised staff report.

Action 11: City council public hearing. The city council holds a decision-making public hearing on the environmental documentation first, then moves on to the amended proposed project.

Action 12: City council action. Finally, the city council makes two decisions: *first*, a decision on the adequacy of the environmental documentation; and *second*, a decision on the proposed project.

DECISION-MAKING PROCESS— ADJUDICATIVE ACTIONS–♥

Action 1: Pre-application conference. The applicant discusses the proposed project with a committee of planning staff members and others. The committee may meet several times.

Action 2: Application submittal. The applicant submits the proposed project for the planner to review.

Action 3: Statutory review period. The planner reviews the proposed project for XX days. During the review, the planner also determines the proposed project's environmental effects and asks that one of the following documents be submitted for review:

- Categorical Exclusion (CATEX)
- Environmental Finding of No Significant Impact (FONSI)
- Environmental Impact Statement (EIS)

Action 4: Planning commission staff report. The planner reviews the proposed project, then writes a staff report that explains the facts in the matter.

Action 5: Planning commission public notice posting. The planner sends the proposed project and the environmental documentation out for public review. The public has XX days to review and comment.

Action 6: Planning commission public hearing packet. The planner sends a packet containing the proposed project, the environmental documentation, any comments received, and the staff report to the planning commission.

Action 7: Planning commission public hearing acting as a decision-making body. The planning commission acts as a decision-making body by holding a public hearing on the proposed project.

Action 8: Planning commission action. Finally, the planning commission makes two decisions: *first*, a decision on the adequacy of the environmental documentation; and *second*, a decision on the proposed project.

DECISION-MAKING PROCESS— STANDARD MINISTERIAL ACTIONS—♥

Note: For a subdivision plat (SDP), the legislative body must make the decision, because as a condition of approval, the subdivider is required to make an irrevocable offer to dedicate real property within the subdivision for streets, alleys, water, drainage and sewers, public utility easements and trails, equestrian trails, and open space. Acceptance or rejection on behalf of the public cannot be delegated to the planning commission or to staff.

Action 1: Pre-application conference. The applicant discusses the proposed project with a committee of planning staff members and others. The committee may meet several times.

Action 2: Application submittal. The applicant submits the proposed project for the planner to review.

Action 3: Decision-making body staff report. The planner reviews the proposed project, then completes a checklist verifying that all legal requirements have been met.

Action 4: Decision-making body public notice posting. The planner sends the proposed project out for public review. The public has XX days to review and comment.

Action 5: Decision-making body public hearing packet. The planner sends a packet containing the proposed project, any comments received, and the checklist verifying that all legal requirements have been met to the planning commission.

Action 6: Decision-making body public hearing acting as a decision-making body. The planning commission acts as a decision-making body by making a decision on the proposed project.

DECISION-MAKING PROCESS—
PECULIAR MINISTERIAL ACTIONS—♥

Note: The building inspector is the decision-maker for three ministerial actions:

- A building permit (BLD) is issued to construct, enlarge, or alter a building.
- A certificate of occupancy (COO) certifies that a building is suitable for occupancy.
- A certificate of compliance (COC) certifies that a real property complies with the state planning and zoning law and local law; it certifies that the lot has been legally created.

Action 1: Pre-application conference. The applicant discusses the proposed project with the building inspector, usually by telephone or email. The parties may interact several times.

Action 2: Application submittal. The applicant submits the proposal to the building inspector to review.

Action 3: Decision-maker notice posting. The building inspector posts a public notice on the site for the duration of the investigation.

Action 4: Decision-maker investigation. The building inspector reviews the proposal, then investigates to verify that all legal requirements have been met or will be met.

Action 5: Decision-maker evidence. The building inspector records an administrative record of the action and files it, verifying that all legal requirements have been met.

PLANNING PERMIT APPLICATION PROCEDURE–♥

This city uses a consolidated planning permit application that allows an applicant to submit a complex proposal as a single action. The consolidated application process is called a "one stop" application procedure. The consolidated planning permit application is made possible by breaking the application into two parts:

- General information
- Specific information

General information. This part asks the applicant to provide name, address, telephone number, and other general information regarding the proposal.

Specific information. This part asks for detailed information, such as layout, design, and parking needs. It is essential for the applicant to submit enough of the right kind of detailed information so staff can write an effective staff report.

STAFF REPORT ANALYSIS

Legislative decisions and adjudicative decisions are processed using similar-looking staff report formats. The main difference between the two is the need to address a finding of fact based on the record of the proceedings.

Downloadable applications and instructions–♥. The city council has the authority to create and administer a full set of downloadable land use regulations, forms, and instructions. All of the necessary application forms and instructions are available on the internet at the jurisdiction's website. Paper application forms and instructions are available at city hall during business hours.

PLANNING PERMIT NOTIFICATION–♥.

Complete public notice must be posted for legislative and adjudicative planning permit applications. Limited public notice is prescribed for ministerial planning permit applications.

Planning permit content of notice–♥. The notice is to contain the following information:

- The hearing date, time, and place.
- The identity of the hearing body.
- A general explanation of the matter to be considered.
- A general description, in text or diagram, of the location of the subject real property

Planning permit posted notice–♥. At least XX days before the public hearing, the city will post a public notice at three prominent locations within the local jurisdiction:

- City hall
- Community center
- Post office

Planning permit mailed notice–♥. At least XX days before a public hearing, notice is to be hand-delivered or mailed to:

- The property owners shown named on the latest equalized assessment role of all real property within XXX feet of the subject real property

- All households residing within the notification boundaries of XXX feet of the subject real property
- The applicant
- The applicant's authorized agent
- Any provider of essential facilities or services, such as schools or utilities
- Neighborhood associations and homeowners associations
- Any person who has requested notification

Planning permit on-site notice–♥. At least XX days before the public hearing, notice is to be posted on the site.

- **Poster material details**. Heavyweight posters, 24" x 36".
- **Placement on lot**. The poster shall be located about two feet back from the property line with the midpoint at breast height (about four feet).
- **Removed or defaced**. If the poster is removed or damaged and remains that way for more than three days, it may need to be reposted to satisfy notification requirements.
- **Posting continuity**. During the posting period, the applicant must inspect the poster once a day to satisfy notification requirements.
- **Visibility from street**. The poster must be clearly visible from the public street.
- **Weatherproof**. The poster must be protected from the weather as needed.
- **Number of posters**. Through-block lots and corner lots require a poster on each street facing exposure.
- **Posting documentation**. The applicant must submit a signed declaration that the posting provisions have been met. Photographic evidence must show the sign posted on the site.

Planning permit newspaper notice–♥. At least XX days before the public hearing, notice is to be published in the newspaper of general circulation having the highest paid circulation within the jurisdiction.

Planning permit mass notice–♥. If the number of property owners who must be notified is greater than 1,000, notice need not be delivered or mailed to individual persons. Rather, a display ad of at least one-eighth (1/8) page is to be published in the newspaper of general circulation having the highest paid circulation within the jurisdiction, at least XX days before the public hearing.

Planning permit mobile home park notice–♥. If a mobile home park is to be converted to another use, notice is to be sent to the tenants of record in the manner specified in the state's planning and zoning law.

Planning permit rental dwelling conversion notice–♥. If the proposal is a conversion of rental dwellings to condominiums, community apartments, or a stock cooperative, notice must be given to the tenants of record in the manner specified in the state's planning and zoning law.

Planning permit failure to receive notice–♥. Failure of any person to receive notice does not invalidate the application, provided that the notice was legally posted.

Chapter 22
LAND USE REGULATIONS–DISTRICTS

In America, separating land into zones reserved for residences or businesses was first applied in mature cities where most of the land had long ago been subdivided into buildable lots. Zoning achieves better results where buildings already occupy existing lots (finished lots).

Where a city has a substantial amount of raw land, zoning has failed to create the nice places where people want to live.

That explains why planners have been tinkering with alternatives to Euclidian zoning—they intuitively know there has to be a better way to improve our quality of life than assigning property to zones. Assigning property to zones has nothing to do with planning—it is more closely related to assigning street address numbers or assessor's parcel numbers (APN).

Another way to look at zoning is to think of it in terms of organizing your wardrobe. You can sort your clothes by season or by color or by function, but no matter how you sort your clothes, if they're from Walmart, Marshall's or Kohl's, they are not going to magically turn into clothes from Oscar de la Renta, Armani, or Loro Piana.

Perhaps zoning districts are just urban clothes hangers dangling real estate price tags.

BUILDINGS, NOT ACTIVITIES

Zoning deals with real estate, not personal property. That is why these land use regulations avoid issuing permits for movable property. Planning permits are issued based on building dimensions and setbacks, not by tenancy—Borders Books, Blockbuster Video, Howard Johnson's, etc.

(AR) ACREAGE RESIDENTIAL ZONING DISTRICT—♦

(AR) Acreage single-family residential district scope—♦. The acreage residential zoning district provides suburban residential size lots for an area that, because of location, distance from some public services, or other developmental factors, is best suited to large lot sizes.

Compatibility. Uses in the zoning district are restricted to those compatible with nearby agriculture, open space, or wildlife habitat.

Criteria. All dwellings must comply with residential-grade construction standards.

(AR) Acreage primary land use—♦. The following land uses are primary uses:

- Single-family dwelling—site-built, manufactured, or modular

(AR) Acreage secondary land uses—♦. The following land uses are examples of secondary uses; their construction requires a building permit (BLD) and a certificate of occupancy (COO):

- Vehicle parking structure
- Structure for in-ground swimming pool, spa, tennis court, and the like
- Stable for horses, ponies, cows, etc.

- Accessory dwelling—a smaller residential dwelling located on the same lot as the single-family home

(AR) Acreage temporary land use–♦. The following land uses are temporary land uses, subject to removal before the certificate of occupancy (COO) may be issued:

- On-site contractor's facilities—office, tool shed, security post, fencing, toilets, and the like
- On-site occupancy during construction—temporary worker or property owner housing in trailers, campers, tents, and the like
- Sales or rental offices, model homes, upgrade displays, sales signs, and the like

(AR) Acreage conditional land use–♦. A conditional use permit (CUP) is required for:

- construction of a residential-grade building on an existing lot (finished lot) where the building cannot comply with lot dimensions, setbacks, lot coverage, or height-limit requirements; or
- construction of a commercial- or industrial-grade building that will be used for:
  - Meetinghouse such as a church, synagogue, temple, mosque, or hall
  - Fraternity such as a lodge or club
  - Board and care or convalescence
  - Child day care or preschool
  - Elementary, high school, or college, business, trade, technical, or similar
  - Country club, stable, golf course, swimming club.

(AR) Acreage building permit–♦. A property owner must obtain a building permit (BLD) prior to the start of construction to prevent a property from being improperly constructed.

(AR) Acreage occupancy permit–♦. A property owner must obtain a certificate of occupancy (COO) prior to occupancy to prevent a property from being used in a way it was not intended.

(AR) Acreage minimum lot area–♦. Minimum lot area is:

- X acres

(AR) Acreage lot dimensions–♦. Minimum lot dimensions in feet are:

- Width, interior lot: XX feet
- Width, corner lot: XX feet
- Depth: XXX feet

(AR) Acreage building setbacks–♦. The minimum building setbacks in feet are:

- Front yard setback: XX feet
- Side yard setback, interior side: XX feet
- Side yard setback, street side: XX feet
- Two stories: add X feet per side
- Rear yard setback: XXX feet

(AR) Acreage maximum lot coverage–♦. Maximum lot coverage by buildings (building footprint):

- XX percent

(AR) Acreage maximum structure height limit–♦. Maximum structure height is:

- XX feet

(LR) LOW-DENSITY SINGLE-FAMILY RESIDENTIAL–♦

(LR) Low-density single-family residential scope–♦. The low-density residential zoning district provides a suitable environment for a family living at a typical single-family residential density.

The low-density zoning district has a full complement of public utilities, neighborhood schools, shopping, and recreation.

Compatibility. Low-density residential neighborhoods need to be designed to promote pedestrians, bicycles, scooters, etc. (The war on skateboards was lost long ago.)

Criteria. All dwellings must comply with residential-grade construction standards.

(LR) Low-density primary land use–♦. The following land uses are primary uses:

- Single-family dwelling—site-built, manufactured, or modular

(LR) Low-density secondary land uses–♦. The following land uses are examples of secondary uses; their construction requires a building permit (BLD) and a certificate of occupancy (COO):

- Vehicle parking structure
- Structure for in-ground swimming pool, spa, tennis court, and the like
- Accessory dwelling—a smaller residential dwelling located on the same lot as the single-family home

(LR) Low-density temporary land use–♦. The following land uses are temporary land uses, subject to removal before the certificate of occupancy (COO) may be issued:

- On-site contractor's facilities—office, tool shed, security post, fencing, toilets, and the like
- On-site occupancy during construction—temporary worker or property owner housing in trailers, campers, tents, and the like
- Sales or rental offices, model homes, upgrade displays, sales signs, and the like

(LR) Low-density conditional land use–♦. A conditional use permit (CUP) is required for:

- construction of a residential-grade building on an existing lot (finished lot) where the building cannot comply with lot dimensions, setbacks, lot coverage, or height-limit requirements; or

- construction of a commercial- or industrial-grade building that will be used for:
  - Meetinghouse such as a church, synagogue, temple, mosque, or hall
  - Fraternity such as a lodge or club
  - Board and care or convalescence
  - Child day care or preschool
  - Elementary, high school or college, business, trade, technical, or similar
  - Country club, stable, golf course, swimming club.

(LR) Low-density building permit–♦. A property owner must obtain a building permit (BLD) prior to the start of construction to prevent a property from being improperly constructed.

(LR) Low-density occupancy permit–♦. A property owner must obtain a certificate of occupancy (COO) prior to occupancy to prevent a property from being used in a way it was not intended.

(LR) Low-density minimum lot area–♦. Minimum lot area is:

- XXX square feet

(LR) Low-density lot dimensions–♦. Minimum lot dimensions in feet are:

- Width, interior lot: XX feet
- Width, corner lot: XX feet
- Depth: XXX feet

(LR) Low-density building setbacks–♦. Minimum building setbacks in feet are:

- Front yard setback: XX feet
- Side yard setback, interior side: XX feet
- Side yard setback, street side: XX feet

- Two stories: add X feet per side
- Rear yard setback: XXX feet

(LR) Low-density maximum lot coverage–◆. Maximum lot coverage by buildings (building footprint):

- XX percent

(LR) Low-density maximum structure height limit–◆. Maximum structure height is:

- XX feet

(MR) MEDIUM-DENSITY RESIDENTIAL ZONING DISTRICT–◆

(MR) Medium-density residential scope–◆. The medium-density residential zoning district provides a suitable environment for a small family living at an increased density, convenient to shopping, entertainment, recreation, and public transit. The medium-density residential zoning district reduces the need for multiple cars per family.

Compatibility. Medium-density residential must incorporate a physical design that imparts a sense of security.

Criteria. All dwellings must comply with residential-grade construction standards.

(MR) Medium-density two-, three-, & four-unit residential primary land use–◆. The following land uses are primary uses:

- Cluster housing—several site-built, manufactured, or modular homes on a single lot
- Duplex, triplex, fourplex apartments on a single lot

(MR) Medium-density secondary land uses–◆. The following land uses are examples of secondary uses; their construction requires a building permit (BLD) and a certificate of occupancy (COO):

- Vehicle parking structure
- Structure for in-ground swimming pool, spa, tennis court, and the like

(MR) Medium-density temporary land use–◆. The following

land uses are temporary land uses, subject to removal before the certificate of occupancy (COO) may be issued.

- On-site contractor's facilities—office, tool shed, security post, fencing, toilets, and the like
- On-site occupancy during construction—temporary worker or property owner housing in trailers, campers, tents, and the like
- Sales or rental office, model home upgrade display, sales signs, and the like

(MR) Medium-density conditional land use–♦. A conditional use permit (CUP) is required for:

- construction of a residential-grade building on an existing lot (finished lot) where the building cannot comply with lot dimensions, setbacks, lot coverage, or height-limit requirements; or
- construction of a commercial- or industrial-grade building that will be used for:
  - Meetinghouse such as a church, synagogue, temple, mosque, or hall
  - Fraternity such as a lodge or club
  - Board and care or convalescence
  - Child day care or preschool
  - Elementary, high school or college, business, trade, technical, or similar
  - Country club, stable, golf course, swimming club.

(MR) Medium-density building permit–♦. A property owner must obtain a building permit (BLD) prior to the start of construction to prevent a property from being improperly constructed.

(MR) Medium-density occupancy permit–♦. A property owner must obtain a certificate of occupancy (COO) prior to occupancy to prevent a property from being used in a way it was not intended.

(MR) Medium-density minimum lot area–♦. Minimum lot area is:

- XXXX square feet

(MR) Medium-density lot dimensions–♦. Minimum lot dimensions in feet are:

- Minimum width, interior lot: XX feet
- Minimum width, corner lot: XX feet
- Minimum depth: XXX feet

(MR) Medium-density building setbacks–♦. The minimum building setbacks in feet are:

- Side yard setback, interior side: XX feet
- Side yard setback, street side: XX feet
- Two stories: add X feet per side
- Rear yard setback: XXX feet

(MR) Medium-density maximum lot coverage–♦. Maximum lot coverage by buildings (building footprint):

- XX percent

(MR) Medium-density maximum structure height limit–♦. Maximum structure height is:

- XX feet

(HR) HIGH-DENSITY RESIDENTIAL ZONING DISTRICT–♦

(HR) High-density multiple-family (five or more unit) residential scope–♦. The high-density residential zoning district provides a suitable environment for a single adult and small family living at a typical urban dwelling density. The high-density residential zoning district has walkable access to shopping, entertainment, recreation, and public transit.

Compatibility. The high-density residential zoning district is a high-intensity activity node. Properties must incorporate physical design that imparts a sense of security

Criteria. All dwellings must comply with residential-grade construction standards.

(HR) High-density primary land use–♦. The following are primary uses:

- Cluster housing—several site-built, manufactured, or modular homes on a single lot
- Duplex, triplex, fourplex apartments on a single lot
- Buildings of five or more dwellings on a single lot

(HR) High-density secondary land uses–♦. The following land uses are examples of secondary uses; their construction requires a building permit (BLD) and a certificate of occupancy (COO):

- Vehicle parking structure
- Structure for in-ground swimming pool, spa, tennis court, and the like

(HR) High-density temporary land use–♦. The following are temporary land uses, subject to removal before the certificate of occupancy (COO) may be issued:

- On-site contractor's facilities—office, tool shed, security post, fencing, toilets, and the like
- On-site occupancy during construction—temporary worker or property owner housing in trailers, campers, tents, and the like
- Sales or rental office, model home upgrade display, sales signs, and the like

(HR) High-density conditional land use–♦. A conditional use permit (CUP) is required for:

- construction of a residential-grade building on an existing lot (finished lot) where the building cannot comply with lot dimensions, setbacks, lot coverage, or height-limit requirements; or
- construction of a commercial- or industrial-grade building that will be used for:

- Meetinghouse such as a church, synagogue, temple, mosque, or hall
- Fraternity such as a lodge or club
- Board and care or convalescence
- Child day care or preschool
- Elementary, high school or college, business, trade, technical, or similar
- Country club, stable, golf course, swimming club.

(HR) High-density building permit–♦. A property owner must obtain a building permit (BLD) prior to the start of construction to prevent a property from being improperly constructed.

(HR) High-density occupancy permit–♦. A property owner must obtain a certificate of occupancy (COO) prior to occupancy to prevent a property from being used in a way it was not intended.

(HR) High-density minimum lot area–♦. Minimum lot area is:

- XXX square feet

(HR) High-density lot dimensions–♦. Minimum lot dimensions in feet are:

- Width, interior lot: XX feet
- Width, corner lot: XX feet
- Depth: XXX feet

(HR) High-density building setbacks–♦. The minimum building setbacks in feet are:

- Front yard setback: XX feet
- Side yard setback, interior side: XX feet
- Side yard setback, street side: XX feet
- Two stories: add X feet per side
- Three stories: add X feet per side
- Rear yard setback: XXX feet

(HR) High-density maximum lot coverage–♦. Maximum lot coverage by buildings (building footprint):

- XX percent

(HR) High-density maximum structure height limit–♦. Maximum structure height is:

- XX feet

(NC) NEIGHBORHOOD COMMERCIAL ZONING DISTRICT–♦

(NC) Neighborhood commercial scope–♦. The neighborhood commercial (NC) zoning district protects the character of the historic downtown and promotes new land uses that seamlessly blend with the look and feel of the historic central business district, which dates from circa 1910.

The neighborhood commercial (NC) zoning district also applies to existing and future neighborhood shopping areas.

In the future, each neighborhood shopping area will be reconfigured to capture the look and feel of the historic central business district, which dates from circa 1910. This means redeveloping single-story strip commercial shopping and replacing it with "downtown-like" urban nodes that incorporate housing and other noncommercial uses. Each new neighborhood shopping area will have its own distinct look and feel. This will lead to a clearly recognizable sense of place. Neighborhood shopping areas should be places where surrounding residents will want to go for socializing as well as shopping.

Convenience. Neighborhood commercial provides goods and services purchased frequently and at fairly regular intervals—food, drugs, hardware, casual clothing; services such as hair care, laundry, and dry cleaning; and quick-serve restaurants, medical offices, and other personal services.

Location. Neighborhood commercial is currently found at free-standing stores and at retail nodes scattered around town. In the future, housing and leisure-time activities will be added as urban density increases.

Compatibility. Neighborhood commercial must be compatible with the surrounding neighborhood and provide easy pedestrian access to customers and nearby residences.

Criteria. All nonresidential buildings must comply with commercial-grade construction standards.

(NC) Neighborhood commercial primary uses–♦. The following are primary uses:

- General sales and services—store, restaurant, hotel, bank, day care facility, mini-storage facility, and the like (Design, not a short-term tenant, is the qualifier.)

(NC) Neighborhood commercial secondary uses–♦. The following land uses are examples of secondary uses; their construction requires a building permit (BLD) and a certificate of occupancy (COO):

- Vehicle parking structure
- Appurtenances such as storage buildings and loading, materials handling, waste disposal structures (cardboard compactors), and the like
- Sign structure

(NC) Neighborhood commercial temporary land uses–♦. The following are temporary land uses, subject to removal before the certificate of occupancy (COO) may be issued.

- On-site contractor's facilities—office, tool shed, security post, fencing, toilets, and the like
- On-site occupancy during construction—temporary worker or property owner housing in trailers, campers, tents, and the like
- Sales or rental office, model home upgrade display, sales signs, and the like

(NC) Neighborhood commercial outdoor land use–♦. Transitory business activities may be conducted in a front yard during business hours:

- The use—including outdoor seating, merchandise display, portable signs, balloon displays, air dancers, feather flags, and the like—must be fenced off from public land. (The city's property department also rents public land for a fee for exhibits, displays, carnivals, circuses, musical events, and the like.)

(NC) Neighborhood commercial conditional land use–♦. A conditional use permit (CUP) is required for:

- construction of a commercial-grade building on an existing lot (finished lot) where the building cannot comply with lot dimensions, setbacks, lot coverage, or height-limit requirements; or
- construction of a commercial- or industrial-grade building that will be used for:
    - Meetinghouse such as a church, synagogue, temple, mosque, or hall
    - Fraternity such as a lodge or club
    - Board and care or convalescence
    - Child day care or preschool
    - Elementary, high school or college, business, trade, technical, or similar
    - Country club, stable, golf course, swimming club
    - Purpose-built vehicle fueling, servicing, and repair buildings.

(NC) Neighborhood commercial building permit–♦. A property owner must obtain a building permit (BLD) prior to the start of construction to prevent a property from being improperly constructed.

(NC) Neighborhood commercial occupancy permit–♦. A property owner must obtain a certificate of occupancy (COO) prior to occupancy to prevent a property from being used in a way it was not intended.

(NC) Neighborhood commercial lot area–♦. The minimum lot area is:

- XXX square feet

(NC) Neighborhood commercial lot dimensions–♦. The minimum lot dimensions in feet are:

- Width, interior lot: XX feet
- Width, corner lot: XX feet
- Depth: XXX feet

(NC) Neighborhood commercial building setbacks–♦. The minimum building setbacks in feet are:

- Front yard setback: XX feet
- Side yard setback, interior side: XX feet
- Side yard setback, street side: XX feet
- Rear yard setback: XXX feet

(NC) Neighborhood commercial maximum lot coverage–♦. In keeping with the land use pattern established during early years, maximum lot coverage by buildings (building footprint) is limited to fifty (50) percent. This custom was established to allow parking and loading between the rear of the building and the rear property line.

(GC) GENERAL COMMERCIAL ZONING DISTRICT–♦

(GC) General commercial scope–♦. The general commercial zoning district provides for the concentration of modern business at nodes accessible from major thoroughfares. The intent is to provide land for unified shopping centers designed and developed as integrated units.

Shopping goods. General commercial provides goods and services that are purchased infrequently, are often expensive, and trigger comparison shopping. Planners refer to these goods and services as shopping goods. Examples include large-screen TVs, fine jewelry, new cars, major appliances, designer furniture, and cell phones. (Design, not a short-term tenant, is the qualifier.)

Hustle and bustle. General commercial is located in the downtown, at scattered big-box retail nodes, or at the mall. General commercial provides a wide variety of wish fulfilment. General commercial benefits from the symbiotic relationship between businesses and customers—the hustle and bustle of human activity.

Compatibility. General commercial must be compatible with the surrounding neighborhood and provide easy pedestrian access to customers, while not degrading nearby residences.

Criteria. All nonresidential buildings must comply with commercial-grade construction standards.

(GC) General commercial primary uses–♦. The following are primary uses:

- General sales and services—store, restaurant, hotel, bank, day care facility, mini-storage facility, and the like

(GC) General commercial secondary uses–♦. The following land uses are examples of secondary uses; their construction requires a building permit (BLD) and a certificate of occupancy (COO):

- Vehicle parking structure
- Appurtenances such as storage buildings and loading, materials handling, and waste disposal structures (cardboard compactors), and the like
- Sign structure

(GC) General commercial temporary uses–♦. The following land uses are temporary land uses, subject to removal before the certificate of occupancy (COO) may be issued.

- On-site contractor's facilities—office, tool shed, security post, fencing, toilets, and the like

- On-site occupancy during construction—temporary worker or property owner housing in trailers, campers, tents, and the like
- Sales or rental office—model interior upgrade displays, sales signs, and the like

(GC) General commercial mandatory noise barrier–♦. If a general commercial site adjoins a residential zoning district, a solid wall noise barrier between the two zoning districts may be required.

(GC) General commercial outdoor use–♦. Transitory business activity may be conducted in a front yard during business hours:

- The use—including outdoor seating, merchandise display, portable signs, balloon displays, air dancers, feather flags, and the like—must be fenced off from public land. (The city's property department also rents public land for a fee for exhibits, displays, carnivals, circuses, musical events, and the like.)

(GC) General commercial conditional land use–♦. A conditional use permit (CUP) is required for:

- construction of a commercial-grade building on an existing lot (finished lot) where the building cannot comply with lot dimensions, setbacks, lot coverage, or height-limit requirements; or
- construction of a commercial- or industrial-grade building that will be used for:
  - Meetinghouse such as a church, synagogue, temple, mosque, or hall
  - Fraternity such as a lodge or club
  - Board and care or convalescence
  - Child day care or preschool
  - Elementary, high school or college, business, trade, technical, or similar
  - Country club, stable, golf course, swimming club

- Purpose-built vehicle fueling, servicing, and repair buildings.

(GC) General commercial building permit–◆. A property owner must obtain a building permit (BLD) prior to the start of construction to prevent a property from being improperly constructed.

(GC) General commercial occupancy permit–◆. A property owner must obtain a certificate of occupancy (COO) prior to occupancy to prevent a property from being used in a way it was not intended.

(GC) General commercial lot area–◆. The minimum lot area is:

- XXX square feet

(GC) General commercial lot dimensions–◆. The minimum lot dimensions in feet are:

- Width, interior lot: XX feet
- Width, corner lot: XX feet
- Depth: XXX feet

(GC) General commercial building setbacks–◆. The minimum building setbacks in feet are:

- Front yard setback: XX feet
- Side yard setback, interior side: XX feet
- Side yard setback, street side: XX feet
- Rear yard setback: XXX feet

(GC) General commercial maximum lot coverage–◆. The maximum lot coverage by buildings (building footprint) is XX percent.

(LI) LIGHT INDUSTRIAL ZONING DISTRICT–◆

(LI) Light industrial scope–◆. The light industrial zoning district provides for the concentration of modern clean industries and aesthetically pleasing structures in industrial parks and along major thoroughfares. The intent is to provide land for unified industrial centers designed and developed as integrated units.

(LI) Light industrial land uses–♦. General characteristics of light industrial land uses:

Unobtrusive. They are land uses that do not attract attention in a way that bothers their neighbors. Light industry includes quiet, non-polluting factories and a wide range of storage. Light industrial land benefits from easy access to workers and proximity to truck, train, and air transport. Light industrial land benefits from symbiotic relationships between businesses that interact regularly with their suppliers—raw materials dealers, wholesalers, and service providers. Light industries typically fabricate, process, or otherwise create products that are later sold to commercial businesses.

Examples of uses. The following are examples of unobtrusive light industrial: buildings and structures designed for manufacture and handling of apparel, jewelry, instruments, computers, appliances, etc., on-site vehicle parking, motor vehicle sales and repair, and "auto row."

Compatibility. Light industrial buildings must be compatible with the surrounding neighborhood and provide easy access to customers and nearby residences.

Criteria. All industrial buildings must comply with industrial-grade construction standards.

(LI) Light Industrial primary uses–♦. The following are primary uses:

- Manufacturing, repair, wholesaling, and the like
- Purpose-built vehicle fueling, servicing, and repair buildings

(LI) Light Industrial secondary uses–♦. The following land uses are examples of secondary uses; their construction requires a building permit (BLD) and a certificate of occupancy (COO):

- Vehicle parking structure
- Appurtenances such as storage buildings and loading, materials handling, and waste disposal structures (cardboard compactors), and the like
- Commercial use buildings built to commercial-grade standards that are compatible with light industrial land uses
- Accessory dwelling located on the same lot, intended for site security
- Sign structure

(LI) Light industrial temporary uses–♦. The following land uses are temporary land uses, subject to removal before the certificate of occupancy (COO) may be issued:

- On-site contractor's facilities—office, tool shed, security post, fencing, toilets, and the like
- On-site occupancy during construction—temporary worker or property owner housing in trailers, campers, tents, and the like
- Sales or rental office—model leased area upgrade display, sales signs, and the like

(LI) Light industrial mandatory noise barrier–♦. If a general commercial site adjoins a residential zoning district, a noise barrier between the two zoning districts is required.

(LI) Light industrial outdoor use–♦. Business may be conducted in a front yard during business hours:

- The use—including outdoor seating, merchandise display, portable signs, balloon displays, air dancers, feather flags, and the like—must be fenced off from public land.

(LI) Light industrial conditional land use–♦. A conditional use permit (CUP) is required for:

- construction of an industrial-grade building on an existing lot (finished lot) where the building cannot comply with lot dimensions, setbacks, lot coverage, or height-limit requirements; or

- construction of a commercial- or industrial-grade building that will be used for:
  - Meetinghouse such as a church, synagogue, temple, mosque, or hall
  - Fraternity such as a lodge or club
  - Board and care or convalescence
  - Child day care or preschool
  - Elementary, high school or college, business, trade, technical, or similar.

(LI) Light industrial building permit–♦. A property owner must obtain a building permit (BLD) prior to the start of construction to prevent a property from being improperly constructed.

(LI) Light industrial occupancy permit–♦. A property owner must obtain a certificate of occupancy (COO) prior to occupancy to prevent a property from being used in a way it was not intended.

(LI) Light industrial lot area–♦. The minimum lot area is:

- XXX square feet

(LI) Light industrial lot dimensions–♦. The minimum lot dimensions in feet are:

- Width, interior lot: XX feet
- Width, corner lot: XX feet
- Depth: XXX feet

(LI) Light industrial building setbacks–♦. The minimum building setbacks in feet are:

- Front yard setback: XX feet
- Side yard setback, interior side: XX feet
- Side yard setback, street side: XX feet
- Rear yard setback XXX feet

(LI) Light industrial maximum lot coverage–♦. The maximum lot coverage by buildings (building footprint) is XX percent.

(LI) Light industrial maximum height limit–♦. Maximum height limit:

- No building or structure shall exceed XX stories or XX feet, whichever is the lesser.

(HI) HEAVY INDUSTRIAL ZONING DISTRICT–♦

(HI) Heavy industrial scope–♦. Heavy industry is essential to the well-being of the community and the economic success of the nation. The heavy industrial zoning district provides for the concentration of obtrusive industries that produce unavoidable smoke, odor, or noise or manufacture or use significant amounts of hazardous chemicals or toxic substances. Heavy industries also include structures that are aesthetically incompatible with residential or commercial land uses. Heavy industry needs to be located where it can safely operate without garnering complaints from neighboring property owners or residents.

Compatibility. Heavy industrial buildings must be shielded from the surrounding neighborhood and provide a high level of security to discourage trespass. Heavy industrial uses can be dangerous to the well-being of the general public

Criteria. All heavy industrial buildings must comply with industrial-grade construction standards.

(HI) Heavy industrial primary uses–♦. General characteristics of heavy industrial:

Obtrusive. Often unpleasant-looking buildings and structures designed for processing chemicals, steel, or oil; manufacturing; batch plants; purpose-built vehicle fueling; servicing; and repair.

Downwind. Often bad smelling—sewage disposal, sanitary land fill, tallow or soap processing, slaughtering.

Ugly. Visually offensive—automobile salvage, recycling, truck repair, boat yards, contractor's yard.

(HI) Heavy industrial secondary uses–♦. The following land uses are examples of secondary uses; their construction requires a building permit (BLD) and a certificate of occupancy (COO):

- Vehicle parking structure
- Sign structure
- Appurtenances such as storage buildings and loading, materials handling, and waste disposal structures (cardboard compactors), and the like
- Commercial use buildings built to commercial-grade standards that are compatible with heavy industrial land uses, such as quick-serve restaurants and convenience stores, to service the nearby workforce
- Accessory dwelling located on the same lot, intended for site security

(HI) Heavy industrial temporary uses–♦. The following land uses are temporary land uses, subject to removal before the certificate of occupancy (COO) may be issued:

- On-site contractor's facilities—office, tool shed, security post, fencing, toilets, and the like
- On-site occupancy during construction—temporary worker or property owner housing in trailers, campers, tents, and the like
- Sales or rental office—model leased area, upgrade display, sales signs, and the like

(HI) Heavy industrial mandatory noise barrier–♦. If a heavy industrial site adjoins a residential zoning district, a noise barrier between the two zoning districts is required.

(HI) Heavy industrial outdoor uses–♦. Transitory business activity may be conducted in a front yard during business hours:

- The use—including outdoor seating, merchandise display, portable signs, balloon displays, air dancers, feather flags, and the like—must be fenced off from public land.

(HI) Heavy industrial conditional land use–♦. A conditional use permit (CUP) is required for:

- construction of an industrial-grade building on an existing lot (finished lot) where the building cannot comply with lot dimensions, setbacks, lot coverage, or height-limit requirements; or
- construction of a commercial- or industrial-grade building that will be used for:
  - Meetinghouse such as a church, synagogue, temple, mosque, or hall
  - Child day care or preschool.

(HI) Heavy industrial building permit–♦. A property owner must obtain a building permit (BLD) prior to the start of construction to prevent a property from being improperly constructed.

(HI) Heavy industrial occupancy permit–♦. A property owner must obtain a certificate of occupancy (COO) prior to occupancy to prevent a property from being used in a way it was not intended.

(HI) Heavy industrial lot area–♦. The minimum lot area is:

- XXX square feet

(HI) Heavy industrial lot dimensions–♦. The minimum lot dimensions in feet are:

- Width, interior lot: XX feet
- Width, corner lot: XX feet
- Depth: XXX feet

(HI) Heavy industrial building setbacks–♦. The minimum building setbacks in feet are:

- Side yard setback, interior side: XX feet
- Side yard setback, street side: XX feet

* Rear yard setback: XXX feet

(HI) Heavy industrial maximum lot coverage–♦. The maximum lot coverage by buildings (building footprint) is XX percent.

(GWOD) GREENWAY OVERLAY DISTRICT–♦

(GWOD) Greenway overlay district scope–♦. The greenway overlay district applies to land bordering the _____ River. To protect the river and the shoreline, a waterway easement facilitates debris and obstruction removal:

* The waterway easement is the XX feet of land that extends into the lot from the lot line that faces the _____ River.

* If granting the waterway easement would prevent development of the lot in compliance with city land use regulations, the city has the option of purchasing the lot or reducing the required lot dimensions to allow development. However, in no case may the required XX-foot waterway easement be waived.

* At the time a vacant lot is developed, a waterway easement is to be dedicated to the city.

* If the primary land use on a developed lot is destroyed, demolished, or removed, the lot is deemed to be vacant for the purpose of dedicating the waterway easement.

(REOD) REDEVELOPMENT OVERLAY DISTRICT–♦

(REOD) Redevelopment overlay district scope–♦. The redevelopment overlay district applies to land that is within a redevelopment project area. The redevelopment overlay district designation may make property eligible for special incentives, such as subsidized rehabilitation, low-interest home improvement loans, grants, and other incentives:

* The redevelopment overlay district allows for rehabilitation of an area without strict adherence to the underlying Euclidean

zoning. The redevelopment overlay district accommodates a mixture of shopping, employment, and housing opportunities not foreseen at the time Euclidean zoning was applied to the project area.

- Any lot or group of lots in a redevelopment overlay district may be developed under regulations that apply to the underlying Euclidean zoning district or under regulations that apply to a planned development overlay district.

(PDOD) PLANNED DEVELOPMENT OVERLAY DISTRICT–♦

(PDOD) Planned development overlay district scope–♦. A planned development proposal allows the property owner to circumvent the exiting Euclidian zoning designation in favor of a development that uses the land in a more creative way. The proposal may include any combination of residential, commercial, and industrial land use. The two-stage planned development permit process is explained below:

- Legislative planning permit: Planned Development Zoning (PDZ) is a legislative planning permit that requires two public hearings—first, before the planning commission serving as an advisory body, then by the legislative body (city council) serving as a decision-making body. The change of zoning is settled by ordinance. It is a lengthy process. Once the decision has been made, the land is given a planned development (PDZ) overlay district number—PDZ numbers run consecutively (1, 2, 3).
- Adjudicative planning permit: Planned development proposal (PDP) permit is an adjudicative planning permit that requires only one public hearing before the planning commission serving as a decision-making body.

Once the planned development zoning (PDZ) is approved, a

planned development proposal (PDP) permit may be issued. (Usually done at the same public hearing.)

The two-part process is recommended because the future is not known to us. If, for any reason, the planned development proposal (PDP) needs to be revised in the future, the changes may be approved at another adjudicative planning permit hearing, without having to go through the lengthy PDZ legislative hearing process.

Planners know from experience that planned development proposals (PDPs) often need to be revised due to market fluctuations, change of ownership, change of mind, etc.

(PAOD) PUBLIC AMENITY OVERLAY DISTRICT–♦

(PAOD) Public amenity overlay district scope–♦. The public amenity overlay district allows for the placement of public amenities that provide for the general welfare of the community and enhance livability. Public amenities may be investor owned or government owned.

- The public amenity land use must be designed to be compatible with surrounding land uses to the maximum feasible extent.
- The public amenity land use must meet the regulations applicable to the zoning district to the maximum feasible extent.
- The public amenity land use must be processed the same way as a similar land use application if feasible.

Examples of public amenity land uses. The following land uses are typical of public amenity land uses:

- Infrastructure for transportation.
- Major public utility structures, such as water wells with pump stations and electric power substations. The category does not include minor public utility structures, such as electric power

poles, telephone poles, fire hydrants, streetlights, and grouped mailboxes.

- Public recreation facilities, such as parks, playgrounds, public swimming, ball fields, ball courts, track and field, and exercise courses.
- Public education facilities, such as libraries, elementary and secondary schools, and special purpose schools.
- Government business offices, such as city hall, law courts, and public safety, city engineer, and planning and building offices.
- A planned government center that may include offices, public safety, national defense, education, and recreation.
- A planned community center that may include education and recreation.

Chapter 23
LAND USE REGULATIONS–STANDARDS

Standards–♣

Standards scope–♣. A standard is a rule or principle that is used as a basis for judgment. Land use regulations include many standards.

The following standards are just placeholders. You will have to come up with your own local standards:

- Architectural standards
- Art in public places standards
- Disability standards
- Engineering standards
- Historic preservation standards
- Landscaping standards
- Outdoor lighting standards
- Park and recreation standards
- Planning Standards
- Subdivision standards

Sources of standards. Many standards are created by the federal government, universities, special interest groups, or professional associations.

For example:

- The International Dark-Sky Association has a "mission to preserve and protect the nighttime environment and our heritage of dark skies through environmentally responsible outdoor lighting."[93]
- HUD Model Manufactured Home Installation Standards. HUD has a mandate to make sure manufactured homes meet certain quality standards.[94]
- Some councils of government produce regional standards as part of their service to member localities.

Stand-alone documents. I highly recommend that standards not be included in the code of ordinances for several reasons:

- Standards can easily run to several hundred pages.
- Standards may be federal guidelines specifically intended for wide use by local governments.
- Standards may be made available for public use under a Creative Commons license.
- Standards may be given away to local governments to promote a special interest group, such as the disabled.
- Standards may be ever changing due to rapid technological or scientific progress.

Availability. Paper format standards should be available to the public at city hall during business hours. Electronic standards should be available to the public from a website. Standards must be available to the public at no cost.

Chapter 24
RE:CODE OR COMMON SENSE

Re:code LA started in 2013 and was scheduled to end in 2017. That's five long years. But it is now 2019, and *re:code LA* is still dragging on. I don't suppose anyone can say for sure when or if it will ever be completed. But from what little that has been made public, I can see that the *re:code LA* product will continue to be massively complicated. Perhaps that's inevitable. I've never tried to plan for a megacity.

I'm a fan of small towns, or at least of neighborhoods and districts that maintain their individuality and sense of place.

SIDE-BY-SIDE COMPARISON:
RE:CODE LA VS. COMMON SENSE ZONING

"[The code] has become this vast, unwieldy system," said Alan Bell, deputy director of the city's Planning Department. "There's a lot of utility in making it more understandable."[103]

I recently received the draft outline of the new land use regulations for the City of Los Angeles. Los Angeles appears to be going down the same path it has been going down since the dawn of time.

Re:code LA Land Use Regulations Outline		
Article 1. Introductory Provisions	Article 6: Use Districts	Article 11. Overlays & Specific Plans
Article 2. Form	Article 7. Citywide Use Standards	Article 12. Administration
Article 3. Frontages	Article 8. Streets & Public Improvements	Article 13. Nonconformities
Article 4. Development Standard Sets	Article 9. Division of Land	Article 14. Measurements, Definitions
Article 5. Citywide Development Standards	Article 10. Incentive Systems	Article 15. Fees

Common sense land use regulations eliminate the unnecessary, condense the essential, and present the code title in only four suits.

Common Sense Land Use Regulations Outline			
Procedures–♠	Permits–♥	Districts–♦	Standards–♣

Chapter 25
TIME FOR A U-TURN

Zoning doesn't do much to improve urban communities. The more I investigated, the more I became convinced that Euclidian zoning and its offshoots have led us down a dead-end street; it's time to make a U-turn.

Land use regulations can't make your community a nice place to live. For that, you need to turn to planning.

A RETURN TO PLANNING

Any of the following planning permits may be used to return zoning to the realm of planning, without disrupting current Euclidian zoning:

Form-Based Code Adoption or Amendment (FBC)

General Plan Adoption or Amendment (GPA)

Specific Plan Adoption or Amendment (SPA)

ZONING-DIRECTED DEVELOPMENT

Both complex zoning and simple zoning restrict creativity and innovation by nitpicking—concentrating on inconsequential details. Applicants who wish to make a major creative change to a property will find themselves stymied by discredited twentieth-century bureaucratic paperwork.

PLANNING-DIRECTED DEVELOPMENT

I believe that if an applicant is given an opportunity to submit a creative application to city hall, chances are that is what the applicant will do.

But faced with a gauntlet of rigid, inflexible, and maladaptive civil servants and the century-old Euclidian land use regulations they have sworn to enforce, applicants usually take the path of least resistance—if cookie-cutter Euclidian zoning is what the rigid, inflexible, and maladaptive want, that is what they will get.

If city hall wants creative development, all it has to do is ask for it.

NIGHTMARE-DIRECTED DEVELOPMENT

Two years ago, my family was forced to relocate to Arizona to seek medical care. When we arrived, we were struck by the virtual absence of city planning.

Eventually we were able to piece together some of what went wrong with planning in Arizona: Spoilers who disdain government in principle saw to it that Arizona's local governments adopted the most primitive form of Euclidian zoning. Consequently, dealing with any Arizona code of ordinances becomes a nightmare excursion into the twilight zone.

At this very moment, all around my community, I see mid-twentieth-century subdivisions sprouting up out of farm fields as far as the eye can see. It looks like 1970s Orange County. (In my nightmares, I see applicants eagerly rolling out cookie dough to be baked into subdivisions.)

I also see the mistakes that ruined much of California: overly wide streets; separation of land uses; pedestrian and bicycle hostility; "remainder land" relegated to parks and single-purpose stormwater retention ponds; no "through-the-block" shortcuts; and sky-glow glare and light trespass.

COMMAND AND CONTROL–DIRECTED DEVELOPMENT

Many jurisdictions are still using improvement standards from the 1970s or even from the 1920s.

Antiquated improvement standards lead to antiquated planning permit applications. The reason so many new real estate developments look so bad is because applicants are forced to build Levittown forevermore. "[U]rban historian Lewis Mumford described the community they constituted as a 'uniform environment from which escape is impossible.'"[95]

Strong Towns adds, " . . . or how many of the things we build are making our communities worse places to live today."[96]

Command and control: The Green Book. The Federal Highway Administration's *Green Book* consists of transportation standards that perpetuate mid-twentieth-century transportation philosophy. *The Green Book* makes "it difficult for cities to design streets that improve pedestrian and bicyclist safety at the expense of vehicle throughput."[97]

Command and control: Fresno. "For the last 40 years, Fresno [California] has required residential streets to have a right of way that is at least 40 feet wide, while arterial streets have a minimum width of 106 feet."[98] I know from my eight years of teaching school in Fresno that walking (actually running) across a 106-foot street is death-defying. (I rode the bus to school—the bus stop was on the far side of a fast-moving arterial.)

Defying command and control: Oregon. The State of Oregon has found that "deaths and injuries to pedestrians increase significantly as the speed of motor vehicles goes up. A typical 36-foot-wide residential street has 1.21 collisions/mile/year as opposed to 0.32 for a 24-foot-wide street. The safest streets were narrow, slow, 24-foot-wide streets."[99]

Since the year 2000, Oregon has been reducing the width of streets to promote safety and encourage peace and quiet in residential neighborhoods.

Defying command and control: San Pablo. One of the first communities I worked in as a planner had very narrow streets—twenty-four feet. The city was conveniently walkable. And by using only 18 percent of the land for streets, housing density soared to twenty-five units per acre—extremely high density for a quiet community of single-family homes.

ADDRESSING INDIVIDUALITY

Recently, I drove by a house similar to mine. It had the same floor plan and also had the same sort of six-foot privacy wall. As I drove by, the householder opened the side yard gate, giving me a view of a backyard full of 1960s muscle cars—a 1967 Shelby Cobra 427 Super Snake, a 1968 Dodge Charger R/T, and a 1969 Chevrolet Camaro ZL1.

When I got home, I walked out to my backyard and counted five citrus trees, four peach trees, two pear trees, two nectarine trees, three apricot trees, two almond trees, seven rose bushes, two rare flowering vines, a row of flowering shrubs, five varieties of tomatoes, a few melons, and all sorts of green vegetables.

We may be neighbors, but we don't seem to have much in common. Yet, Euclidian zoning assumes we do and treats us both the same.

Much of planning and zoning has to do with individual taste. That is why it is so difficult for planners to satisfy people's needs while being held captive by the laws of physics and the utilitarian properties of the built environment.

There are very real reasons why so many good intentions go so wrong; it's not always someone's fault—it's the nature of trying to look into the future. Zoning is a primitive tool lacking the sophistication needed to address an ever-changing world.

MASLOW'S HIERARCHY OF NEEDS

The great psychologist Abraham Maslow postulated that humans have five needs that must be satisfied in order to live a satisfying life.[100]

Basic Human Needs	
Physiological needs	Breathing, circulation, temperature, intake of food and fluids, elimination of wastes, movement
Safety and security needs	Housing, community, climate
Love and belonging needs	Relationships with others, communications with others, support systems, being part of community, feeling loved by others
Self-esteem needs	Fear, sadness, loneliness, happiness, accepting self
Self-actualization needs	Thinking, learning, decision-making, values, beliefs, fulfillment, helping others

Euclidian zoning cannot address these basic human needs—planning can.

Chapter 26
LOCAL PLAN SOLUTION

As a matter of practicality, and just like private businesses, governments should formulate and maintain four interdependent levels of plans:

FIRST LEVEL: GENERAL PLAN

Traditionally, city planners refer to the first-level plan as the general plan or the comprehensive plan, but it is similar to the strategic plan a business would have.

The first-level plan paints a picture of what the city should look like in the future. A well-crafted first-level plan should present a picture of what the city should look like at full development and at some intermediate point, usually twenty years in the future.

I use the term "picture" because, in most cases, a city's first-level plan is a color-coded map showing the location of future land uses.

The color-coded land use map looks simplistic to most people, but to a professional city planner, it provides a wealth of spatial information, in a snapshot, that would take reams of paper to express; or, as they say: "A picture is worth a thousand words."[101]

In a first-level plan for a city, most of the accompanying text elaborates on the land use map by explaining the reasoning behind the allocation of each color shown on the map and by the pattern of the color-coded mosaic.

The first-level plan also presents policies that ensure that the city will grow as depicted on the land use map.

The first-level plan should be strong enough to control the way property development will take place over the long run, while being flexible enough to accommodate unforeseen contingencies.

As a matter of practicality, a city needs a first-level plan that

- establishes the path of growth;
- estimates the rate of population growth;
- calculates the percentage of land needed for each type of land use;
- schedules the installation date for new public utilities and services;
- forestalls potential land use conflicts; and
- establishes aesthetic standards as a component of land use governance.

The first level customarily applies to the entire land area of the city and any land beyond its borders that may eventually be annexed.

The first-level plan should define the maximum land area and the maximum population of the city. If it doesn't (and most don't), the city will not be able to effectively plan for the proper sizing of roads, pipes, wires, public buildings, or other utilities and facilities that must be designed for a defined population or land area based on a known formula or ratio.

Failure to define population or land area parameters leads to endless rounds of premature infrastructure failure and expensive resizing, such as our unending expansion of urban freeways.

SECOND LEVEL: INTERMEDIATE PLAN

City planners traditionally refer to the second-level plan as a community or neighborhood plan. The second-level plan applies to a smaller land area than a first-level plan and contains more detail. The second-level plan may also have a shorter time frame and focus on a more limited goal.

The second-level plan supports the first-level plan by concentrating on a distinct land area or government function, such as the siting of police substations, firehouses, parks and playgrounds, or underground utilities.

THIRD LEVEL: SPECIFIC PLAN

It is common for a city to have several intermediate plans. City planners refer to the third-level plan as a specific plan or focused plan. Most specific plans are written for redevelopment projects or for planned unit developments.

The third-level plan gives detailed directions for every aspect of land use development, from building design to infrastructure capacity. It is a detailed plan, or a blueprint.

The third-level plan should answer four questions:

- Where are we now?
- Where do we want to be?
- How do we get there?
- How do we measure our progress?

The third-level plan works best if it follows the straightforward principles embodied in the SMART formula.[102]

SMART is an acronym for the five steps that lead to a goal:

- **Specific**. The goal must be well-defined and focused.
- **Measurable**. The goal must be measurable, using mileposts that quantify progress.
- **Assignable**. The work program must show who will complete the tasks.
- **Realistic**. The work program must show how resources will be allocated to reach the goal.

- **Time-based**. The work program must show the list of events needed to reach the goal in chronological order.

The SMART formula forces the city to incorporate accountability into the third-level plan.

The third-level plan, because it leads to physical land development, must contend with the legal concept of operational risk—that is, the risk of failure caused by human error, fraud, breach of security or privacy, engineering failure, or ecological mishap.

Higher-level plans (first- and second-level plans), are low-risk paper plans, but the third-level plan leads to physical action. The third-level plan cannot be fixed with an eraser—it must be carefully thought out ahead of time, with all risks taken into consideration.

FOURTH LEVEL: EMERGENCY PLAN

The fourth-level plan plots out the course of action that needs to be followed if the preferred plan fails or the assumed future changes. Not many governments develop effective fourth-level plans. After all, what could possibly go wrong? Flood, fire, earthquake, drought . . .

Chapter 27
CONCLUSION AND DOWNLOADS

As soon as I heard that Los Angeles was initiating a process called *re:code LA,* I felt obligated to involve myself as much as possible. I was intrigued by the amount of time and money involved: five years and $5 million. (Now, after seven years and who knows how much money, *re:code LA* is still a work in progress.)

That's a lot of time and money to ordinary people like me. I thought to myself, there has to be a less expensive alternative, so I set out determined to find a quicker and cheaper way to write land use regulations.

Now I ask, after two years of effort, have I met the challenge? Is common sense zoning something worth trying?

Too much. I've ended up with much too much to put in this book, so I've posted the odds and ends on the internet. You may download those bits and pieces from my website: http://common-sensezoning.com

Downloads:
- Mail merge forms and data files;
- In-house planning permit processing forms;
- Instructions for applicants; and
- Free advice, for whatever it's worth.

ENDNOTES

1   Carolyn Kellogg, "La-La-Land Now in the Dictionary," *Los Angeles Times*, March 25, 2011. Accessed June 29, 2015, http://latimesblogs.latimes.com/jacketcopy/2011/03/la-la-land-now-the-dictionary-definition-of-l os-angeles.html#sthash.Yyz0KhR7.dpuf.

2   "Growth in Urban Population Outpaces Rest of Nation, Census Bureau Reports," United States Census Bureau, March 26, 2012. Accessed June 29, 2015, https://www.census.gov/newsroom/releases/archives/2010_census/cb12-50.html.

3   "Quick Facts, Los Angeles City, California," United States Census Bureau. Accessed July 11, 2019, https://www.census.gov/quickfacts/fact/table/losangelescitycalifornia#viewtop.

4   *Recommendation Report*, Department of City Planning, CPC-2014-1582-CA, A-2, Project: *re:code LA*, City of Los Angeles, May 22, 2014. Accessed August 24, 2019, http://cityplanning.lacity.org/Code_Studies/ReformCodeStudies/FinalEvalStaffRpt.pd.

5   "Quick Facts, Los Angeles California Population," United States Census Bureau, 2010. Accessed July 11, 2019, https://www.census.gov/quickfacts/fact/table/losangelescitycalifornia#viewtop.

6   "Quick Facts, Fresno California Population," United States Census Bureau, 2010. Accessed July 11, 2019, https://www.census.gov/quickfacts/fact/table/fresnocitycalifornia/PST045216#viewtop.

7   William Strunk, Jr., and E. B. White, *The Elements of Style*, 4th ed. (United Kingdom: Longman, Harlow, 1999).

8   "The Challenges of Re:Coding L.A.," City of Los Angeles, December 9, 2013. Accessed June 29, 2015, http://recode.la/updates/news/challenges-recoding-la.

9   Amanda Erickson, "The Birth of Zoning Codes, a History," Citylab, Jun 19, 2012. Accessed July 11, 2019, https://www.citylab.com/equity/2012/06/birth-zoning-codes-history/2275/.

10   Ibid.

11   City of New York Board of Estimate and Apportionment Building Zone Resolution. Accessed July 11, 2019, (Adopted July 25, 1916.)

12   "Syllabi and Course Materials, URBP 225: Land Use Planning and Law," Urban & Regional Planning, San José State University, College of Social Sciences. Accessed July 11, 2019, http://www.sjsu.edu/urbanplanning/courses/index.html#u225.

13   "Quotes About Superficiality," Goodreads. Accessed July 11, 2019, http://www.goodreads.com/quotes/tag/superficiality.

14   Margaret Rouse, "Systems Thinking," SearchCIO. Accessed July 11, 2019, http://searchcio.techtarget.com/definition/systems-thinking.

15   "PAS Reports," American Planning Association. Accessed July 11, 2019, https://www.planning.org/pas/reports/.

16   James Longtin, "Longtin's California Land Use 2d" (two-volume hardbound set and current update). Accessed August 24, 2019, http://longtinslanduse.com/order.html

17   Daniel J. Curtin, Jr., and Cecily T. Talbert, *Curtin's California Land Use and Planning Law,* 27th ed. (Point Arena, CA: Solano Press, 2007).

18   L. Frank Baum, "Pay no attention to the man behind the curtain," *The Wizard of Oz.* Accessed July 11, 2019, https://www.goodreads.com/quotes/92087-pay-no-attention-to-the-man-behind-the-curtain.

19   *Annual Report,* Department of City Planning, City of Los Angeles, 2016. Accessed July 11, 2019, https://planning.lacity.org/Documents/Exec/2016_AnnualReport.pdf.

20   Who We Are, September 30, 2019, email Sent to Connor Murphy from yeghig.keshishian@lacity.org

21   "Pareto principle," Wikipedia. Accessed July 11, 2019, https://en.wikipedia.org/wiki/Pareto_principle.

22   "What's Happening in Planning," Los Angeles Department of City Planning, July 2013. Accessed July 11, 2019, http://cityplanning.lacity.org/ Reorganization/Planning2013.pdf.

23   Andrew Pulver, "Chinatown," *The Guardian*, October 22, 2010. Accessed July 11, 2019, https://www.theguardian.com/film/2010/oct/22/ best-film-ever-chinatown-season.

24   "Mapping L.A.," *Los Angeles Times*. Accessed July 11, 2019, http://maps.latimes.com/neighborhoods/neighborhood/list/.

25   Andy Bowers, NPR News. Accessed July 11, 2019, http://www.npr.org/ news/specials/la/secession/.

26   Ibid.

27   Ibid.

28   "I'd be the biggest man in the country." Scene 11, The Day the Earth Stood Still (1951) *https://www.amazon.com/Day-Earth-Stood Still/dp/B00005JKFR/ ref=sr_1_1?crid=CZX436HOFK02&keywords=the+day+the+earth+stood+still+ 1951+dvd&qid=1563907700&s=movies-tv&sprefix=the+day+ %2Cgarden%2C241&sr=1-1*

29   "Economies of scale," Wikipedia. Accessed July 11, 2019, https://en.wikipedia.org/wiki/Economies_of_scale.

30   Wendell Cox and Joshua Utt, "The Costs of Sprawl Reconsidered: What the Data Actually Show," *https://www.heritage.org/report/the-costs-sprawl-reconsidered- what-the-data-really-show*

31   Wendell Cox, "America Is More Small Town than We Think," New Geography, 09/10/2008, *https://www.newgeography.com/content/ 00242-america-more-small-town-we-think*

32   Ibid.

33   Wendell Cox, "America Is More Small Town than We Think," NewGeography, September 10, 2008. Accessed December 31, 2017, http:// www.newgeography.com/content/00242-america-more-small-town-we-think.

34   Ibid.

35   "Village of Euclid v. Ambler Realty Co.," Wikipedia. Accessed July 11, 2019, https://en.wikipedia.org/wiki/Village_of_Euclid_v._Ambler_Realty_Co.

36   Malvina Reynolds, "Little Boxes," 1962. Accessed July 11, 2019, https://
en.wikipedia.org/wiki/Little_Boxes.

37   Lane Kendig, *Performance Zoning* (Chicago: APA Planners Press, 1980).

38   "Form-Based Codes Defined," Form-Based Codes Institute. Accessed
July 11, 2019, https://formbasedcodes.org/definition/.

39   Daniel G. Parolek, AIA, Karen Parolek, Paul C. Crawford, FAICP,
*Form Based Codes: A Guide for Planners, Urban Designers, Municipalities,
and Developers* (Hoboken, NJ: John Wiley & Sons, 2008).

40   "The Planner's Guide to Specific Plans," Governor's Office of Planning and
Research. Accessed (January 2001), http://www.opr.ca.gov/docs/specific_plans.pdf.

41   "Form-Based Codes Defined," Form-Based Codes Institute. Accessed
July 11, 2019, https://formbasedcodes.org/definition/.

42   "Ancient Land Law: Title Insurance in Mesopotamia," Punctual Abstract,
February 16, 2018. Accessed July 11, 2019, https://www.punctualabstract.com/
2018/02/16/ancient-land-law/.

43   "Honduras country profile," BBC News Services, May 16, 2018. Accessed
July 11, 2019, https://www.bbc.com/news/world-latin-america-18954311.

44   "Planning & Zoning Procedures," Nance County, Nebraska, 1999. Accessed
July 11, 2019, http://www.co.nance.ne.us/pdfs/zoning/regulations/procedures.pdf.

45   "Periodic table," Wikipedia. Accessed July 11, 2019, https://en.wikipedia.
org/wiki/Periodic_table.

46   Roger Bernhardt and Ann M. Burkhart, *Property*, 6th ed. (St. Paul, MN:
West, 2012). Accessed July 11, 2019, https://lscontent.westlaw.com/images/
content/Property6th.pdf.

47   Email from BBuchanan@concordtownship.org.

48   "Edmond Hoyle," Wikipedia. Accessed July 11, 2019, https://en.wikipedia.
org/wiki/Edmond_Hoyle.

49   City of Glendale, Arizona, Code of Ordinances, May 22, 2019,
https://library.municode.com/az/glendale/codes/code_of_ordinances

50   Ibid.

51   City of Phoenix, Zoning Ordinance, Chapter 4 Planning Documents, Section 403 Specific plans, D Review and hearing procedure, 4. a. Accessed September 27, 2019. https://www.phoenix.gov/citygovernment/codes

52   Sara Vincent, Best practice sentence length: why 25 words is our limit, 4 August 2014, Accessed Sep 27, 2019, https://insidegovuk.blog.gov. uk/2014/08/04/sentence-length-why-25-words-is-our-limit/

53   Natalie Wexler, "Why Americans Can't Write," *Washington Post*, September 24, 2015. Accessed July 11, 2019, https://www.washingtonpost.com/opinions/why-americans-cant-write/ 2015/09/24/6e7f420a-6088-11e5-9757-e49273f05f65_story.html.

54   *Merriam-Webster*, s.v. "gobbledygook." Accessed July 11, 2019, https://www.merriam-webster.com/dictionary/gobbledygook.

55   "Law and Requirements," PlainLanguageLaw.gov. Accessed July 11, 2019, https://www.plainlanguage.gov/law/.

56   Google search for "what is the literacy rate in the United States." Accessed July 11, 2019, https://www.google.com/search?rlz=1C1CHBF_ enUS829US829&q=what+is+the+literacy+rate+in+the+united+states&sa= X&ved=2ahUKEwjYlNmXlKPiAhVRoFsKHXbyAnkQ1QIoAnoECAoQAw& biw=1920&bih=937.

57   Phoenix City Code, Code Publishing Company, Seattle, Washington, A Codification of the General Ordinances of the City of Phoenix, Arizona, 2019, Section 600 General Provisions. *https://www.codepublishing.com/AZ/Phoenix/*

58   William C. Burton, *Burton's Legal Thesaurus*, 4E. Accessed July 11, 2019, https://legal-dictionary.thefreedictionary.com/personal+property.

59   "Working from Home? Consider the Home Office Deduction," IRS, Tax Tip 2011-53, March 16, 2011. Accessed July 11, 2019, https://www.irs.gov/uac/Work-From-Home%3F-Consider-the-Home-Office-Deduction.

60   "Cottage Industry," Investopedia. Accessed July 11, 2019, https://www.investopedia.com/terms/c/cottage-industry.asp.

61   Wal-Mart Stores, Inc. v. City of Turlock, 483 F. Supp. 2d 987 (E.D. Cal. 2006)

62   John Holland, "Court Upholds Superstore Ban in Turlock, CA," Reclaim Democracy, First published by the *Modesto Bee*, December 22, 2004. Accessed July 11, 2019, http://reclaimdemocracy.org/walmart_turlock_ban_upheld/.

63   "North American Industry Classification System," Wikipedia. Accessed July 11, 2019, https://en.wikipedia.org/wiki/North_American_Industry_ Classification_System.

64   City of San Bernardino, Planning Commission Agenda, February 19, 2014.

65   "Blockbuster LLC," Wikipedia. Accessed July 11, 2019, https://en.wikipedia.org/wiki/Blockbuster_LLC.

66   The Top Resource for Franchise Opportunities Worldwide, https://www.franchise.org/

67   According to livability.com, January 2018. Accessed July 11, 2019, https://www.google.com/search?q=themed+towns+in+usa&rlz=1C1CHBF_ enUS829US829&oq=theme+towns&aqs=chrome.4.69i57j0l5.16003j1j8 &sourceid=chrome&ie=UTF-8.

68   Adrian Mourby, "Where are the world's most war-damaged cities?," *The Guardian*, December 17, 2015. Accessed July 11, 2019, https://www. theguardian.com/cities/2015/dec/17/where-world-most-war-damaged-city.

69   Tenth Amendment to the United States Constitution, https://en.wikipedia. org/wiki/Tenth_Amendment_to_the_United_States_Constitution

70   Police power (United States constitutional law). Accessed August 24, 2019, https://en.wikipedia.org/wiki/Police_power_(United_States_constitutional_law). Accessed August 24, 2019,

71   Ibid.

72   Ibid.

73   Governor's Office of Planning and Research, A Citizens Guide to Planning, State of California, January 2001. Accessed August 24, 2019,*https://web.archive. org/web/20150511210104/http:/ceres.ca.gov/planning/planning_guide/plan_index. html%23anchor193958#anchor175423*

74   Superior Court of Delaware, New Castle County. WAWA, INC., Appellant v. NEW CASTLE COUNTY BOARD OF ADJUSTMENT, Appellee. Civil Action No. 04A-05-005-JOH. Decided: January 10, 2005. Accessed August 24, 2019,

75   California Planning Guide: An Introduction to Planning in California, Governor's Office of Planning and Research, Sacramento, December 2005 Edition. Accessed August 24, 2019, http://web2.co.merced.ca.us/pdfs/commissionarchive/2010/6-23-2010/california_planning_guide_an_introduction_to_planning_in_ca.pdf

76   1999 Land Use Law Update, Timothy Bates, Esq., OSP Annual Planning and Zoning Conference, May 22, 1999. Accessed August 24, 2019.

77   *John R. Harrington & a. v. Town of Warner*, 152 N.H. 74, 81 (2005); see also *Farrar v. City of Keene*, No. 2008-500, slip op. at 4 (N.H. May 7, 2009). Accessed August 24, 2019,

78   "New Hampshire Town and City," NHMA, July/August 2010. Accessed August 24, 2019,

79   Ibid

80   Municipal Law Lecture Series, Lecture Two, *The Five Variance Criteria in the 21st Century*, 2009. Accessed August 24, 2019, https://www.nh.gov/osi/resource-library/zoning/documents/the-five-variance-criteria-in-the-21st-century.pdf.

81   David W. Owens and Adam Bruggemann, *A Survey of Experience with Zoning Variances*, School of Government (North Carolina: UNC Chapel Hill, 2004). Accessed August 24, 2019, http://sog.unc.edu/sites/www.sog.unc.edu/files/full_text_books/zonvar.pdf.

82   James F. Scales, Practical Advice for Variances, Mika Meyers PLC. Accessed August 24, 2019, *https://www.mikameyers.com/news/article/practical-advice-for-variances*

83   "Evidentiary Standards and Burdens of Proof," Justia. Accessed August 24, 2019, https://www.justia.com/trials-litigation/evidentiary-standards-burdens-proof/.

84   *Drum v. Fresno County Public Works*, 144Cal. App. 3D 777, 782 (1983).

85   http://www.sjsu.edu/urbanplanning/docs/URBP229Materials/NoviVCityPacifica.pdf.
http://vjel.vermontlaw.edu/files/2013/07/Regulating-Big-Box-Stores-The-Proper-Use-of-the-City-or-Countys-Police-Power-and-its-Comprhensive-Plan-Californias-Experience.pdf

86   uslegal.com, https://municipal.uslegal.com/police-powers/
protection-public-health-safety-morals/

87   Colin Ellard, "The Generic City," *Slate*, November 27, 2015. Accessed July
11, 2019, http://www.slate.com/articles/health_and_science/science/2015/11/
psychology_of_boring_architecture_the_damaging_impact_of_big_ugly_
buildings.html.

88   Jacoba Urist, "The Psychological Cost of Boring Buildings," *The Cut*,
April 12, 2016. Accessed July 11, 2019, https://www.thecut.com/2016/04/
the-psychological-cost-of-boring-buildings.html.

89   Curtin and Talbert, op. cit.

90   Daniella Cheslow, "U.S. Slips In Annual Global Corruption Rankings,"
NPR, January 29, 2019. Accessed July 11, 2019, https://www.npr.org/
2019/01/29/689639808/u-s-slips-in-annual-global-corruption-rankings.

91   Tim Worstall, "Bribery and Corruption in the Planning System—So, Make
the Planning System Simpler, Dolts," Adam Smith Institute, May 2018. Accessed
July 11, 2019, https://www.adamsmith.org/blog/bribery-and-corruption-in-the-
planning-system-so-make-the-planning-system-simpler-dolts.

92   "Why Were You Interested in Serving on Your Planning Commission?"
PlannersWeb, October 6, 2014. Accessed July 11, 2019, http://plannersweb.com/
2014/10/interested-serving-planning-commission/.

93   The International Dark-Sky Association. Accessed July 11, 2019,
https://www.darksky.org/about/.

94   *Model Manufactured Home Installation Standards*, 2003 ed. Accessed July 11,
2019, https://www.hud.gov/sites/documents/225HUD.PDF.

95   "Levittown, the prototypical American suburb—a history of cities in
50 buildings, day 25," *The Guardian*, April 28, 2015. Accessed July 11, 2019,
https://www.theguardian.com/cities/2015/apr/28/levittown-america-
prototypical-suburb-history-cities.

96   Strong Towns. Accessed July 11, 2019, https://www.strongtowns.org/about.

97   John Urgo, Meredith Wilensky, and Steven Weissman, *Moving Beyond Pre-
vailing Street Design Standards: Assessing Legal and Liability Barriers to More Efficient
Street Design and Function* (Berkeley: University of California, 2011). Accessed July
11, 2019, https://www.law.berkeley.edu/files/4.1_CREC_codes_and_standards.pdf.

98   Ibid.

99   *Neighborhood Streets Project Stakeholders, Neighborhood Street Design Guidelines: An Oregon Guide for Reducing Street Widths,* Stakeholder Design Team, 2000. Accessed July 11, 2019, https://www.oregon.gov/lcd/Publications/NeighborhoodStreetDesign_2000.pdf.

100   "Maslow's hierarchy of needs," Wikipedia. Accessed July 11, 2019, https://en.wikipedia.org/wiki/Maslow%27s_hierarchy_of_needs.

101   "A picture is worth a thousand words," Wikipedia. Accessed July 11, 2019, https://en.wikipedia.org/wiki/A_picture_is_worth_a_thousand_words.

102   "SMART criteria," Wikipedia. Accessed July 11, 2019, https://en.wikipedia.org/wiki/SMART_criteria.

103   Tim Logan, "L.A. is working on major zoning code revamp," JULY 30, 2014, Accessed October 10, 2019, https://www.latimes.com/business/realestate/la-fi-zoning-code-revamp-20140731-story.html.

Made in the USA
Coppell, TX
02 June 2021